God's  Heal You

by A.A. Allen

For more great Christian classics that have been out-of-print for far too long, visit us online at:

JawboneDigital.com

ISBN: 1984023942
ISBN-13: 978-1984023940
Copyright © 2017 Jawbone Digital
Yuma, Colorado

TABLE OF CONTENTS

CHAPTER 1
GOD'S GUARANTEE TO HEAL YOU

The prayer of faith shall save the sick, and the Lord shall raise him up (James 5:15).

These signs shall follow them that believe; In my name...they shall lay hands on the sick, and they shall recover (Mark 16:17–18).

I am the Lord that healeth thee (Exodus 15:26).

God's Word should never be doubted, because God cannot lie. Whatever God has spoken He is able to make good. Not only is God able to make it good, but His Word declares that He shall make it good. God is not a man that he should lie; neither the son of man that he should repent: hath he said, and shall he not do it? Or hath he spoken, and shall he not make it good? (Numbers 23:19).

God will turn this old world upside-down and inside-out before He will allow one of His promises to fail.

Any person deserves to be trusted until he proves that he is untrustworthy. Surely no one could be more worthy of trust than God, for He always keeps every promise. This all-powerful, unchanging God has promised to heal ALL thy diseases. This is not hope-so, think-so, or may-be-so. It is a definite promise. It is the plain, emphatic Word of God.

Bless the Lord, O my soul, and forget not all his benefits: Who forgiveth ALL thine iniquities; who healeth ALL thy diseases (Psalm 103:2–3).

Believe God's promises

God heals all manner of diseases. Whatever your sickness may be, it is one that God has promised to heal. God has promised to forgive your sins, and He's promised to heal your diseases...and GOD CANNOT LIE.

Many are the afflictions of the righteous: but the Lord

delivereth him out of them ALL (Psalm 34:19). This is another glorious promise from the lips of Him who sits in the heavens.

Can God break a covenant, or alter the thing that has gone out of His lips? NO! A million times NO! My covenant will I not break, nor alter the thing that is gone out of my lips (Psalm 89:34). God will never alter these promises to read, "Who healeth PART of thy diseases," or, "the Lord delivereth him out of a FEW of his AFFLICTIONS." God will do exactly what His promises say. He will deliver you out of ALL afflictions and heal EVERY sickness.

The Lord declared, I am the Lord that healeth thee (Exodus 15:26). If the Lord healed His people yesterday, then He still heals His people today, for God has not changed. Jesus Christ the same yesterday, and to day, and forever (Hebrews 13:8). We know what He will do tomorrow by the things that He did yesterday. The Christ who healed yesterday is the Christ who heals today.

When Jesus said, These signs shall follow them that believe, did He mean what He said? Absolutely! Positively! He meant EXACTLY what He said! He promised, In my name shall they cast out devils; they shall speak with new tongues; they shall take up serpents; and if they drink any deadly thing, it shall not hurt them; THEY SHALL LAY HANDS ON THE SICK, AND THEY SHALL RECOVER (Mark 16:17–18). God promises that when the believer lays hands upon you, you shall recover from ALL your sicknesses and diseases! God means exactly what He says. You shall recover. It shall be done!

Can God lie? No! So just believe it, receive it, and IT SHALL BE DONE.

Stand upon God's promise...memorize it...quote it. Repeat it again and again to yourself, until it lives in you - until you actually believe it. And when you BELIEVE it, you will RECEIVE it.

God will perform His Word

God says, I will hasten my word to perform it (Jeremiah 1:12). God stands behind His Word with all the power in heaven and earth. The God, who spoke this world into existence and hung it upon nothing, says that He will hasten to perform His Word. He will stand behind His promises with all His mighty power. Nothing can prevent God from, keeping His promises, or standing behind the words He has spoken. This is, literally, a GUARANTEE from the lips of God! It is a guarantee to heal you of ALL your diseases, all your sicknesses, and all your afflictions. No guarantee was ever backed by greater power or faithfulness. But no guarantee can be enforced unless the terms of the guarantee have been met. Nothing is ever guaranteed unless it is used according to directions or "taken as directed."

The promises are broad and free. They are for YOU, if you will believe them, accept them, and act upon them.

Again and again, we have been thrilled by the sight of people being healed of all manner of diseases, as they claimed God's promises as their own. As we humbly claimed God's promise to the believer and laid our hands upon the sick, painful and terrifying diseases (many of long standing) have either disappeared instantly, or began to mend from that hour. We have seen the same results in the ministry of many others who have dared to believe that God meant what He said.

But some have gone away sorrowful. They came hoping to receive what others were receiving, but nothing happened. Why? Because they failed to realize the importance of meeting all of God's conditions. They either failed to find out what was expected of them in order to receive healing, or they just didn't think it really mattered very much whether they followed instructions or not.

You must follow the directions

Many people go to a doctor with their troubles. When he gives them two or three bottles of pills with complicated instructions (a pink one every two hours, a white one three times a day, and a gray one at bed time), plus a strict diet and a bottle of something else to rub on - how carefully they follow all the instructions! They hope that all of this will give at least a little relief, but if it does not, they will try something else!

But when God himself guarantees that you WILL recover completely if you will follow instructions, surely it is worth taking time to find out what these instructions are. If you follow them as carefully as a doctor's prescription, your healing cannot fail!

The following lessons/chapters present the instructions God has given in His Word for those who need healing. Do you want to be healed? God wants it for you, even more. If you follow these instructions carefully, God Himself guarantees your healing. Read them carefully and prayerfully. Obey them sincerely and faithfully. Accept God's promises simply, just as you accept the promises of a trusted friend. If you do this, you can start rejoicing NOW, for your healing.

CHAPTER 2
INSTRUCTIONS TO THE SICK

Take fast hold of instruction; let her not go: keep her; for she is thy life (Proverbs 4:13).

Your healing—yes, even your very life—may depend entirely upon the way you take hold of the instruction in this and the following chapters. No doubt countless thousands who are now in their graves would be enjoying perfect health today if they could have received proper instruction about divine healing. There are perhaps millions whose lives are wasting away with disease at this very moment who will never be healed unless they receive proper instruction.

Lack of faith is often the result of lack of instruction. At Nazareth, even Christ himself could...do no mighty work (Mark 6:5). All He was able to do was to lay His hands on a few sick folk and heal them. He marveled because of their unbelief. No doubt the reason for their unbelief was their lack of proper instruction. Christ saw their need and went round about the villages, teaching (Mark 6:6).

God has placed teachers in the Church as one of the ministry gifts (see 1 Corinthians 12:28), yet few people realize the benefits of good instruction and teaching. Many who travel for miles to attend a divine healing campaign become indignant when they are required to attend a meeting for preparatory instruction before they get in the healing line. Many who attend the instruction meetings fail to grasp the instruction they need because they are only attending in order to get in the healing line. Beneficial instruction is given but their hearts are closed to it. These people do not realize the value of such instruction. In many cases, those with little faith have not received proper instruction, either because it was not offered or because they failed to accept it when it was given. On the other hand, almost without exception, those who exercise real faith, believe God's promise, and receive healing are the ones who have taken time for instruction.

Hear instruction, and be wise, and refuse it not (Proverbs 8:33).

Build your faith

Many people have been afflicted for years and have had many outstanding men of God lay hands on them and pray for their healing. And yet they have not received their healing. These people seem to think that all they need to do in order to be healed is to get in a healing line and have someone lay hands on them and pray. They hope that it may be their lucky day. But healing is not a matter of luck. It is a matter of faith—faith in the unchanging and unchangeable Word of God. Without question, these people need appropriate instruction. All scripture is given by inspiration of God, and is profitable for...instruction (2 Timothy 3:16). Those who desire healing should obtain all available instruction - not just in order to get in a healing line, but to build their faith so they can receive of God the things which He said should be theirs. Without faith it is impossible to please him (Hebrews 11:6). Since faith cometh by hearing, and hearing by the word of God (Romans 10:17), those who seek healing should fill their heart with God's promises concerning healing. Read portions of the Bible that will build your faith - the Book of Acts and the Gospel of Mark. Read and memorize as many verses as possible. Study the mighty miracles of healing in these books, and notice how your faith increases. When the tide of your faith has risen and doesn't waver, then it is time to enter the healing line. Then, and only then, can you receive healing.

Get rid of hindrances

We will have a class in this course entitled, "Hindrances to Faith." Read and re-read this material, carefully and prayerfully, until every hindrance has been removed. Search the Word of God. God will speak to the sincere, honest, openhearted individual through His Word. As new light is shed upon your pathway, God expects you to walk in that light, for with new light comes new responsibility. You must be a doer of the Word and not a hearer only. Search your heart and see if there be any wicked way in you. If God reveals sin in your life, you must repent of it immediately. Turn loose of it—drop it as though it were a hot iron! Do not be satisfied to merely prune off the big sins. Prune off every little sin along with the big ones.

Prayer and fasting

Prayer and fasting should be an important part of your preparations for healing. Throughout both the Old and New Testaments of the Bible, we find that the great men of God were those who prayed and fasted. God's power was manifested in their lives and they worked miracles and healed the sick.

Christ himself taught fasting as well as prayer. When the disciples failed to heal a boy who was possessed with a demon, Jesus said to them, This kind can come forth by nothing, but by prayer and fasting (Mark 9:29). God has chosen a fast. It is described in Isaiah 58:6. Is not this the fast that I have chosen? to loose the bands of wickedness, to undo the heavy burdens, and to let the oppressed go free, and that ye break every yoke? The reward of this fast is seen in verse eight of the same chapter. Then shall thy light break forth as the morning, and thine health shall spring forth speedily as the morning, and thine health shall spring forth speedily.

Yet fasting is not a "charm" by which healing can be purchased. Do not boast about your fasting, for Jesus gives these instructions on the matter: Moreover when ye fast, be not, as the hypocrites, of a sad countenance: for they disfigure their faces, that they may appear unto men to fast. Verily I say unto you, They have their reward. But thou, when thou fastest, anoint thine head, and wash thy face; That thou appear not unto men to fast, but unto thy Father which is in secret: and thy Father, which seeth in secret, shall reward thee openly (Matthew 6:16–18). If a person's fasting is directed toward God, he will not boast to others about it, making sure they know of his sacrifice. Those who make such boasts will receive little or nothing from their efforts!

If you have not yet been filled with the Holy Spirit, begin now to seek God for the baptism of the Holy Spirit. It is possible that whatever has prevented you from being filled with the Holy Ghost may also be preventing you from receiving healing. It is evident that those who are filled with the Spirit are able to touch God more quickly than those who have not been filled. Don't be discouraged if you are unable to attend a healing service. God made proper provision for those who are bed-ridden and cannot get into a healing line God wrought special miracles by the hands of Paul: So that from his body were brought to the sick handkerchiefs or aprons, and the diseases departed from them, and the evil spirits went out of them (Acts 19:11–12). If you are one who cannot attend a healing service, contact someone who prays the prayer of faith and ask him or her to send you an anointed handkerchief. (Be sure to read the special section on "Miracles by Handkerchiefs and Aprons" in chapter 11.)

Walk in fellowship with God

When ye stand praying, forgive, if ye have ought against any: that your Father also which is in heaven may forgive you your trespasses (Mark 11:25). An unforgiving spirit—a rebellious heart, refusing to walk in the light of God's Word—is the murderer of faith, which John calls "confidence." Only God's Word can bring real confidence. For those who desire this confidence and faith it is extremely important to walk obediently in the full light of God's Word. To have confidence in God, you must have real fellowship with God. You cannot have real fellowship with God unless you walk in the light of His Word.

Those who walk in darkness cannot have fellowship with God. In fact, they can't even be sure that the blood of Christ cleanses them from sin. This then is the message, which we have heard of him, and declare unto you, that God is light, and in him is no darkness at all. If we say that we have fellowship with him, and walk in darkness, we lie, and do not the truth: But if we walk in the light, as he is in the light, we have fellowship one with another, and the blood of Jesus Christ his Son cleanseth us from all sin (1 John 1:5–7). We can only have real fellowship with Christ when we are doers of the Word and not hearers only. Those who have the greatest fellowship with God are those who have the greatest faith. Those who have the least fellowship with Him are those who have little or no faith. Our faith is in exact proportion to the fellowship, which we have with God. It's no wonder that many today have little faith, for they have very little fellowship with the Lord Jesus Christ. Indeed, many have no fellowship with Him because of a rebellious spirit, or self-will. They refuse to walk in the light of God's Word as it is shed upon their pathway, either through reading and studying it, or through hearing it preached by full-gospel ministers who believe and teach the Word in its entirety.

Without real fellowship with God, there can be no real faith in Him. Continuing in darkness after receiving the light of God's Word will break that fellowship and, according to 1 John 1:7, the blood of Jesus Christ will no longer continue to cleanse us from sin. So rebellion, or self-will, will close the door of your heart to real faith and, at the same time, will open it to doubt and unbelief.

Does God's Word work today?

Christ himself, speaking of the very day in which we live, asked the question, When the Son of man cometh, shall he find faith on the earth? (Luke 18:8). He knew that faith could not live in the atmosphere of modernism, unbelief, doubt, coldness, indifference, and skepticism that prevails today. We need to consider why we don't see more people healed today. Instead of faith in the hearts of men, we find men's hearts failing them for fear (Luke 21:26). Paul, speaking of these last days and the condition of the apostate church, said, For the time will come when they will not endure sound doctrine; but after their own lusts shall they heap to themselves teachers, having itching ears; And they shall turn away their ears from the truth, and shall be turned unto fables (2 Timothy 4:3–4). Would you expect to find faith in such an atmosphere? Never! Paul continues, Having a form of godliness, but denying the power thereof. FROM SUCH TURN AWAY (2 Timothy 3:5).

Thousands of people today attend churches where modernist preachers declare that the day of miracles is past and that Christ does not heal today. They no longer believe that the supernatural, signs following, and the miraculous gifts of the Spirit are for the Church today. They preach beautiful sermons that appeal to the intellect but never touch the heart. They teach that if Christ heals today, He heals through medical science.

Ask one of these modernist preachers if he believes the Bible, and he will say, "Yes, part of it." He will explain that he does not believe in the part that borders on the supernatural. Those modernists believe all that corresponds with reason, but refuse to believe that which they cannot reason out. They reject anything supernatural. They refuse to accept the baptism of the Holy Spirit, speaking in tongues, and the supernatural gifts of healing and miracles. They are modernists to the core. Many of them deny the deity of Christ, the inherent wickedness of man, the blood atonement, and the inspiration of the Bible. Instead of preaching a direct creation, they teach that man is a product of evolution. They do not preach the fall of man, or that man's heart is depraved. Instead, they insist that getting better and better. When they should be preaching salvation by the blood of Christ, they talk of works and character. Instead of preaching the Bible as the inspired Word of God, they teach the theories of science.

These modern preachers would make a mere teacher of our Savior. They do not believe nor do they preach, supernatural regeneration. Rather, they teach "natural development." When they should preach divine sanctification, they talk about "education." Instead of preaching supernatural grace, they lecture on natural "morality."

Could a person exposed to this kind of doctrine week after week have much faith in the supernatural doctrine of healing? Positively not! If a person is to receive healing, it will be because he has faith in the supernatural power of God—not because he doubts it.

God's advice under these circumstances is FROM SUCH TURN A WAY! (2 Timothy 3:5). If you want to have real faith, attend a church where faith is taught and exercised! If you want healing, turn away from those who oppose it and identify yourself with people who believe it. Go to a church where people are encouraged to believe ALL the promises of God and NOT where they are told, "It is not for today."

Gifts of healing...working of miracles

For to one is given by the Spirit...the gifts of healing...To another the working of miracles (1 Corinthians 12:8–10). It is well for those seeking healing to understand that there is a difference between the gifts of healing and the gift of miracles. Ordinarily, the gifts of healing remove the cause of the disease that is injuring the body, and the person regains his health. In some cases, relief will be complete and instant, but many times a state of convalescence begins. This is not a theory, but is thoroughly documented in the Scriptures. Many hearings of Christ were accomplished in just this way—for example, note the healing of the nobleman's son in John 4:46–52.

The gifts of healing do not ordinarily replace a missing organ that may have been removed by surgery or lost in an accident. Healing will restore sight to a blind eye, but if the eyeball is missing then only a miracle could bring sight again. A new eyeball would have to be created and only a miracle could bring about such a new creation. The gifts of healing will restore hearing to deaf ears, but in the case where there are no ear drums, only a miracle can re-create ear drums. A miracle is the setting aside of the ordinary laws of God governing a specific case, such as the sun being made to stand still at the command of Joshua.

Healing is God's promised provision for ALL the sick among His people. A miracle covers only a specific case. God, who created a universe by His Word, can, and sometimes does, recreate missing organs, when there is sufficient faith. God can do anything - all things are possible with Him. But you must understand that the gifts of healing were not intended to take the place of the gift of miracles in the Church. If this were so, the gift of miracles would not be necessary.

The gifts of healing were not intended to make an old person young again. As a person gets older, his body shows signs of aging. The face becomes wrinkled, hair turns gray and may fall out, energy is diminished, and the bodily processes become slower. More rest and careful selection of a proper diet is required in order to maintain good health. However, this does not mean that the aged must suffer from disease. God's promises to His people are good to the end of life.

The gifts of healing do not eliminate death. Until Jesus comes, It is appointed unto men once to die (Hebrews 9:27). The last enemy that shall be destroyed is death (1 Corinthians 15:26). However, death need not be accompanied by horrible sufferings from diseases that God has promised to heal.

Healing was not intended to take the place of the natural processes of life, such as development of mind or stature. Some time ago, a young man twenty-four years of age came into the healing line. He was no more than four feet tall, had the voice of a child, and there was no sign of whiskers on his face. It was very apparent that his condition was abnormal, for both his parents were above the average height and build. Healing would not grow this man a beard in a moment, nor would healing make him a six-footer in the twinkling of an eye. However, healing would strike at the root of the trouble and, after a while, that fellow would have to buy himself a razor and some larger clothes.

Healing will not cause the person who has been deaf

and mute from birth to immediately understand and speak a language that he has never heard. He must learn to speak very much as he would have learned to speak as a child. The process may be more rapid due to more mature mental development. However, he may never speak the language as perfectly as he would have if he had learned to speak at the normal time in life.

Do not be discouraged and don't accuse God of failing or refusing to heal you simply because your healing is not immediately manifested in completion or as a miracle. Take God at His word. Accept your healing as an accomplished fact. It was not accomplished today - or last week. It was accomplished at the whipping post in Jerusalem, on the day that Jesus atoned for your sins. It was not accomplished today - but it is accepted today, and is effective in your life, as you follow the instructions of the Word of God for your deliverance. It is working even now, and will continue to work in your life until you are in perfect health - fully delivered from sickness and sin by the atoning work of Christ!

CHAPTER 3
IS IT GOD'S WILL TO HEAL YOU?

Millions of people who are sick or afflicted today could be enjoying perfect health! Perfect health is in God's carefully laid plan for their lives. He purchased their healing—at great cost to Himself—and made it avoidable for the asking.

Many of these suffering people are people who pray a great deal. They have prayed for healing again and again. Many have passed through healing lines in some of the greatest healing meetings under some of the most effective healing ministries of our time, and yet they are not healed. They pray much, but receive little.

Some prayers for healing are not sufficient to bring deliverance. According to James 1:6–7, one must not only ask, but must ask in faith, nothing wavering. For he that wavereth is like a wave of the sea driven with the wind and tossed. For let not that man think that he shall receive any thing of the Lord.

The person who prays for healing, adding the words, "If it be thy will," is openly confessing to the Lord that he is not at all sure he will receive healing. The "if" in the petition denotes doubt. This type of prayer cannot possibly be classified as asking "in faith, nothing wavering." Praying this way for one's healing is a waste of time, for God said very plainly, Let not that man think that he shall receive anything of the Lord! (James 1:7).

Remove the "if"

There is only one way to take the "wavering" out of your asking—take the "if" out of your petition. You must be convinced that it is the will of God to heal you! Until you are fully convinced of this, real, unwavering faith cannot exist. There will always be doubt about whether or not you will be healed. In fact, you cannot even be assured that God has heard your prayer until you are sure that you have prayed according to His will. For this is the confidence that we have in him, that, if we ask any thing according to his will, he heareth us (1 John 5:14).

How, can we ask without wavering when we, are not even sure that God is listening? Surely we don't expect God to answer prayers which He has never even heard!

Not until we are sure that God has heard our prayer, and we know our petition has met with His approval—that it is according to His will—can we ask "in faith, nothing wavering."

Until you ask in faith, unwavering, you cannot receive! But if you have faith...nothing shall be impossible unto you (Matthew 17:20). When you do ask in faith, heaven itself guarantees the answer!

Before you pray for healing, go to God's Word and learn whether or not it is His will to heal you. If it is not

His will, don't ask Him to do it! Don't waste time saying meaningless prayers that won't be heard in heaven. But if it is God's will to heal you, then leave the "if" out of your petition. Come to God in perfect confidence with unwavering faith and receive your healing!

And this is the confidence that we have in him, that, if we ask anything according to his will, he heareth us: And if we know that he hear us, whatsoever we ask, we know that we have the petitions that we desired of him (1 John 5:14–15).

Listen to the Word of the Lord!

Beloved, I wish above all things that thou mayest prosper and be in health, even as thy soul prospereth (3 John 2). This verse clearly tells us that it is the will of God for His children to be in health. Since it is His will for us to be in health, it cannot—at the same time—be His will for us to be sick! It is God's will to heal you!

The leper of Mark 1:40 must have been somewhat doubtful about the will of God concerning his case, for he besought Him, saying, If thou wilt, thou canst make me clean. But it didn't take long for him to find the will of God. Jesus promptly answered, I will; be thou clean (Mark 1:41).

God wills to heal the sick! If He wills to heal one, then He wills to heal anyone - everyone. He wills to heal YOU. For there is no respect of persons with God (Romans 2:11).

In James 5:14, God asks, Is any sick among you? To whom is He referring? He refers to any person who is sick! ANY—the same word He used when He said He is not willing that ANY should perish but that ALL should come to repentance (2 Peter 3:9). If salvation is for all who will repent, then healing is for all who will believe and act upon God's promise in James 5:14–15. Is any sick among you? Let him call for the elders of the church; and let them pray over him, anointing him with oil in the name of the Lord:

And the prayer of faith SHALL save the sick, and the Lord SHALL raise him up!

Bless the Lord, O my soul, and forget not all his benefits; Who forgiveth all thine iniquities; who healeth all thy diseases (Psalm 103:2–3). These benefits are for both soul and body—salvation and healing! Christ forgives ALL sins and He heals ALL diseases! So don't just remember some of His benefits, but claim all of them. Healing is the will of God for you!

In the beginning, God said, Let us make man in our image, after our likeness...So God created man in his own image, in the image of God created he him; male and female created he them (Genesis 1:26–27). God's creation was strong, powerful, handsome, clean, pure, and healthy! And it is God's will that his creation remain the way He made them—healthy, clean, and pure.

Satan was jealous of God's pure and healthy creation, and wasn't satisfied until he had made his way into the Garden of Eden. When he entered, two unclean spirits followed him in—sin and sickness. Through disobedience to God, mankind lost his purity and became sinful. Then he lost his health and was susceptible to sickness. The double curse of sin and sickness is the result of man's disobedience to God.

Was man ever redeemed from sin? You say, yes! The majority of professing Christians of all faiths will tell you that Christ died upon the cross to redeem mankind from sin. However, many of these same people fail to recognize that when He was crucified, He also took man's sicknesses upon himself and supplied redemption for the body as well as the soul.

A Double Cure For A Double Curse!

As Christ stepped from His heavenly throne in glory to redeem the world from the double curse of sin and sickness, two angels of light and hope followed Him. They were salvation and healing—a double cure!

The Son of God was manifested, that he might destroy the works of the devil (1 John 3:8). The works of the devil are sin and sickness. So God came to destroy not just one, but both. He came to save you and heal you!

Isaiah 53:4,5 says, Surely he hath borne our griefs, and carried our sorrows. Matthew 8:17 quotes the prophecy of Isaiah 53, Himself took our infirmities, and bare our sicknesses. 1 Peter 2:24, also quoting from this prophecy, declares, Who his own self bare our sins in his own body on the tree...by whose stripes ye were healed. It is clear that Christ bore both sin and sickness for us. If He bore them, then we need not bear them. For if we must remain sick, the sufferings of Jesus were in vain.

To clinch the matter, we go back to Isaiah 53:5. But he was wounded for our transgressions, he was bruised for our iniquities: the chastisement, of our peace was upon him; and with his stripes we are healed. This verse was written before Calvary. Peter, looking back to Calvary, says, "By whose stripes ye were healed" (1 Peter 2:24). Accept this redemption and the works of the devil will be destroyed. Every sin will be blotted out and every pain, sickness, and disease will vanish! Satan cannot legally afflict you with that which Christ has already borne for you. Tell the devil so! Believe God for deliverance now!

Under the law, sickness and disease recognized as the curse for disobedience. Moses quotes God as saying, If thou wilt hearken to the voice of the Lord thy God, wilt do that which is right in his sight, and wilt give ear to his commandments and wilt keep all his statutes, I will put none of these diseases upon thee, which I brought upon the Egyptians: for I AM THE LORD THAT HEALETH THEE (Exodus 15:26). Deuteronomy lists every sickness and plague which God said should come upon the people under the law as a result of disobedience. Consumption...fever...inflammation...extreme burning...botch...emerods...scab...itch...madness [insanity]...blindness...astonishment of heart [known today as "nervous breakdown"]. And, then, so none may be overlooked, every sickness, and every plague, which is not written in the book of this law, them will the Lord bring upon thee, until thou be destroyed (Exodus 28:22,2–28,61). This is the curse of the law. But you have been redeemed from the curse of the law! Christ hath redeemed us from the curse of the law, being made a curse for us: for it is written, Cursed is every one that hangeth on a tree (Galatians 3:13).

You are redeemed!

It is the will of Satan, not the will of God, for people to be sick. This is a proven fact, for when Satan is banished from the earth, there will be no more sickness, pain, or tears.

God wants us to live, not die! According as his divine power hath given unto us all things in to life (2 Peter 1:3). It is the will of God for us to be partakers of His divine nature, which is health, and strength, and holiness. Whereby are given unto us exceeding great and precious promises: that by these [the promises you have been reading, and many, many more] ye might be partakers of the divine nature (2 Peter 1:4).

Nevertheless, before you can receive any benefit from these precious promises you must make them your own. You must claim them, believe them, and stand firmly upon them, refusing to believe any argument which Satan may bring against them. Satan will give no ground until you make it very plain to him that he can hold that ground no longer.

About 1500 B.C., God promised, If thou wilt diligently hearken to the voice of the Lord thy God, and wilt do that which is right in his sight...I will put none of these diseases upon thee, which I have brought upon the Egyptians; for I am the Lord that healeth thee (Exodus 15:26). We know that nearly three million people enjoyed perfect health, by obedience and faith in this promise, for we read Psalm 105:37, There was not one feeble person among their tribes.

Much religious teaching today would make God merely the once-great "I was." But Hebrews 13:8 says, "Jesus Christ IS the same yesterday, and to day and for ever." And Malachi 3:6 says, "I am the Lord, I change not." So, if He has never changed, He is still the great "I AM." By believing God's promises, God's people can still be as healthy and strong today as His people were in 1500 B.C. We are still serving the same God, but under a better covenant, which was established upon better promises (Hebrews 8:6). The three million people who came out of Egypt all believed God's promise. There was not one feeble person! They were all strong and well! They believed that, if the promise was for one, it was for all. If it wasn't for all, then it wasn't for anyone.

The reason so many millions remain sick today is because they refuse to believe these wonderful promises:

And he cast out the spirits with his word, and healed all that were sick (Matthew 8:16).

And Jesus went about all the cities...healing EVERY sickness and EVERY disease among the people (Matthew 9:35).

And great multitudes followed him, and he healed them all (Matthew 12:15).

God anointed Jesus of Nazareth with the Holy Ghost and with power: who went about doing good, and healing ALL that were oppressed of the devil; for God was with him (Acts 10:38).

Healing was God's will for His people before Jesus came to earth. It was His will for them during the time of Christ's earthly ministry. And it is God's provision for His people TODAY!

Accept it—NOW!

I have asked many people who came to me, asking prayer for their bodies, "Is God going to heal you?" and received the answer, "I know He is able, if it is His will."

19

These precious people believe (though they cannot back up their belief with scripture), that they are being allowed to suffer to bring patience or long-suffering to their lives. Many believe that sickness may be keeping them in the will of God, or that it may be for the glory of God. Some feel that their sickness is an evidence of God's love toward them. Others feel that God is chastening them through sickness. Yet they insist they do not know why they are being chastened. It never seems to occur to them that they might be able to free themselves of the chastening, by correcting a fault in their lives.

Will a wise and loving father punish his child over a long period of time, refusing to let him know the reason for the punishment? And will not a wise, loving, and obedient son turn immediately from his sin, in order to please the father, and avoid further punishment from the same fault? If sin has separated you from God, so that He cannot hear your prayer, repent now, and God will hear your prayer and heal you. Believe God now for your healing.

Others coming to me for prayer say, "I want to be healed, but if this isn't God's time, then I'll just have to suffer until it is God's own 900 time to heal me."

If it is right for the suffering to wait patiently and endure their sicknesses until some other time in God's perfect will, then it would also be proper to tell the sinner that he cannot be saved today, but must be patient and wait in his sins until it is God's time to save him. Nonsense! Behold, NOW is the accepted time, behold NOW [today] is the day of salvation (2 Corinthians 6:2). If salvation is for all, then healing is for all. It is for YOU! NOW! TODAY is the day God wills to set you free from sin and sickness. Settle it here and now! It is God's Word! God WANTS to heal you NOW! Believe it! Receive it!

Don't ever again be guilty of praying, "Heal me, if it be Thy will."

Raise a hand to heaven now and say, "Jesus, I am so glad that it is Your will to heal me now."

Ask in faith, nothing wavering, and deliverance is yours!

CHAPTER 4
CAUSES OF SICKNESS

For this cause many are weak and sickly among you (1 Corinthians 11:30).

It is a well-known fact that, when a good physician starts to work on a case, the first step is to find out, if possible, the cause of the sickness. Then he works to eliminate that cause. So it is when we come to God for healing. We find that He deals not so much with symptoms as with causes.

It is important to know the causes of sickness. The pain of an attack of acute appendicitis may be eased by administering narcotics. But, while the person is unaware of pain, the appendix may burst and death may result. Carelessness about finding the cause of suffering has resulted in great damage and even the loss of lives. Many people have lost confidence in God's promises to heal, failing to understand that there are conditions that must be met before healing can occur. They fail to remove the cause of sickness and thus fail to meet God's conditions for healing.

God points out in His Word some very specific reasons for sickness. By checking the Word, those who desire to be healed may remove the causes of sickness.

Sin causes sickness

It may be said without fear of contradiction that, in a very real sense, sin is the cause for the existence of sickness in the world. There was no sickness in the Garden of Eden, and none of us expect to find either sin or infirmity in heaven. Until the day Eve yielded to the suggestion of Satan and took of the fruit, which God had forbidden her to eat, the human race was free from both sin and sickness. At that point, Sin entered into the world, and death by sin; and so death passed upon all men, for that all have sinned (Romans 5:12). In this sense all sickness is the result of sin.

In some cases, a specific disease is directly traceable to a specific sin. Perhaps the best examples of this are the so-called "social diseases" which haunt those who live immoral lives. In many other cases, the connection is not so readily apparent, especially to those who cannot discern the things of the Spirit of God. But God said, If thou wilt NOT observe to do all the words of this law...then the Lord will make thy plagues...great plagues and of long continuance, and sore sicknesses, and of long continuance. Moreover he will bring upon thee all the diseases of Egypt, which thou wast afraid of...Also every sickness, and every plague, which is not written in the book of this law, them will the Lord bring upon thee (Deuteronomy 28:58–61).

Sin and sickness are closely associated in the New Testament, as well as in the, Old, for Jesus Himself said, in dealing with sickness, Son, thy sins be forgiven thee (Mark 2:5), and to another, Sin no more, lest a worse thing come unto thee (John 5:14).

James admonishes the, sick, Confess your faults one to another, and pray one for another, THAT YE MAY BE HEALED, and if he have committed sins, they shall be forgiven him (James 5:15–16).

David, speaking by inspiration of the Holy Ghost, said, Fools because of their transgressions, and because of their iniquities, are afflicted. Their soul abhorreth all manner of meat; and they draw near unto the gates of death. Then they cry unto the Lord in their trouble, and he saveth them out of their distresses. He sent his word, and healed them (Psalm 107:17–20).

This should be sufficient evidence that with sin comes sickness. But there is more.

Numbers, chapter 12, presents a story, which brings God's people a very solemn warning. Miriam, Moses' sister, a prophetess and one who had been greatly blessed of the Lord, became lifted up with pride, and was not afraid to speak against [God's] servant, Moses (verse 8). God heard her evil speaking, and "the anger of the Lord was kindled" against Miriam and Aaron, her brother, who had entered with her into the criticism against Moses. Miriam became leprous, white as snow, and would have remained so had not Moses prayed for her deliverance. How marvelous that God heard the cry of Moses and healed Miriam! But note that Miriam would never have needed healing had she not sinned.

Criticism Is Sin!

Sin breaks down the hedge that God builds around you, thus permitting Satan to afflict you.

God, who has pronounced just judgments upon the disobedient, has also given many precious promises of physical well-being to those who will diligently hearken to His voice and do that which is right in His sight. In the Ten Commandments, there is a special promise of long life to those who honor their parents. Honor thy father and thy mother; which is the first commandment with promise; That it may be well with thee, and thou mayest live long on the earth (Ephesians 6:2). If all is not well with thee (physically), could your sickness be the result of breaking this commandment?

If thou wilt diligently hearken to the voice of the Lord thy God, and wilt do that which is right in his sight, and wilt give ear to his commandments and keep all his statutes, I will put NONE of these diseases upon thee, which I have brought upon the Egyptians: for I am the Lord that healeth thee (Exodus 15:26).

Obedience brings healing

Can you believe that God meant what He said? Obedience brings healing! Disobedience brings disease and sickness. The unsaved and disobedient, must prepare for healing by getting right with God!

Paul deals very specifically with the subject of sickness among Christian people in I Corinthians II - He tells us in verse 30, For this cause many are weak and sickly among you, and many sleep (die prematurely). This verse states very clearly that there is a definite cause for Christians' sicknesses. We should give this careful consideration and make sure that we know and understand what this "cause" is.

First Corinthians 11 deals with one of the most important and perpetual ordinances of the Church, the Lord's Supper. Instituted by God the same night, in which He was betrayed, this ordinance became to the followers of Jesus the visible symbol of all He has purchased for us salvation through the shedding of His blood and healing through His sufferings at the whipping post. It is so essential to the believer's life to become a partaker of these sacrifices that Jesus himself said, Except ye eat the flesh of the Son of man, and drink his blood, ye have no life in you (John 6:53).

Yet added to this solemn warning is another, found in 1 Corinthians 11:27–29, Whosoever shall eat this bread, and drink this cup of the Lord, unworthily, shall be guilty of the body and blood of the Lord. But let a man examine himself, and so let him eat of that bread, and drink of that cup.

Worthy or unworthy?

Many professing Christians have refused to take the Lord's Supper because of this warning. However, this was not the Lord's intention. If you are unworthy to partake of the symbols of His blood and body, surely you cannot be a partaker of His blood and body in reality. In that case, Jesus says, Ye have no life in you. If you are unworthy to partake of the communion, you may not be ready for the Rapture.

Worthiness does not imply that one is sure he has fully attained the goal of sinless perfection. Christ himself served the first communion to twelve men who very quickly demonstrated that they were still subject to human weaknesses and were short of perfection.

You say, "Then, what does it imply?"

This word worthiness has a three-fold implication. First, is simply the attitude of the believer at the time he partakes of the symbols. Surely there should never be any frivolity or irreverence at such a solemn time. Never should it be approached lightly or treated as a mere formal ceremony. In partaking of these emblems, we shew the Lord's death till he come (1 Corinthians 11:26). This worthy attitude is by no means a proud spirit or feeling worthy or superior to other men, but rather it is a realization of inherent sinfulness and the deep need of a Redeemer.

The other two implications are embodied in the latter part of verse 29, which is an explanation of the word unworthily - not discerning the Lord's body. The blood of the Lord was shed for the remission of sins, but it was His body that bore the stripes whereby we are healed. Many drink the wine with happy realization and praise to God for the glorious deliverance from sin through His shed blood. But they eat the bread without realizing that this also typifies a definite price that was for a definite blessing. This blessing is HEALING—and it is ours if we will but accept it!

Only as we believe and accept the blood of Christ for salvation do we find salvation. Drinking the wine of the communion, alone, will not wash away our sins. A young man who had been brought up in a home where God's Word was not read, and who was kept busy with things other than church matters, went to church with a friend on communion Sunday. For the first time in his life he saw people taking communion. Very little explanation was made and, when the elements of communion were passed and his friend took a portion, he joined in, just as he would have shared in the treats at a party. He had no realization of the meaning of either the wine or bread and there was no change in his life as a result of taking communion. There must first be an inward understanding of the cleansing of the blood before the outward form can have any meaning.

Many fine Christian people receive no more benefit from partaking of the bread and wine than this boy did-and for the same reason. They have never learned that when Christ our Passover [was] sacrificed for us, that the blood was sufficient to deliver from death, and that the body was provided for healing and physical strength. Because they do not expect healing, they do not receive it.

When the death angel passed over the houses of Israel, he was not concerned with what was on the table or pantry shelf, for God had said, When I see the blood, I will pass over you. Thus the blood set the condemnation to death aside. But the command of God was not completed with the applying of the blood to the door posts, for God had also commanded that they should eat the flesh on that night and thereby receive strength for the journey which lay ahead.

Even so, the blood of Christ shed upon Calvary is fully sufficient to make atonement for our sins. This being true, His sufferings at the whipping post and in Pilate's judgment hall were sufferings all in vain, unless we accept healing. But those sufferings were not in vain!

Christ...suffered for us...Who his own self bare our sins in his own body on the tree, that we, being dead to sins, should live unto righteousness: by whose stripes ye were healed (1 Peter 2:21,24).

As we discern by faith the power of the blood of Christ, we are set free from the guilt and bondage of sin. And, as we discern the body of the Lord, there need not be any weak and sickly among us. The people of Israel accepted both the body and blood of their Passover lamb and, when God brought them forth out of the land of Egypt, there was not one feeble person among their tribes

(Psalm 105:37).

Many churches today, if they were consistent with what they believe, would use only the wine for communion. They believe in the blood for salvation, but reject the broken body for our healing. No wonder so many people are sick. They have refused the only remedy that is guaranteed to cure every disease if used according to directions!

But perhaps the reason the minds of so many have been unable to grasp this glorious truth will be found in the third phase of unworthiness. This is failure to discern the body of the Lord, which is living and active in the world today. Now ye are the -body of Christ, and members in particular. Because of failure to recognize this fact, many have been guilty of causing division in the Body. This is sin and sin kills faith. Therefore, in taking communion, we, as Christians should examine ourselves in light of our relationship to the other members of the Body, as set forth in 1 Corinthians 12, not belittling any person or any gift placed by the Spirit of Christ in His body. Both spiritual and physical welfare depend largely upon this right responsibility in the body of Christ. If you have been guilty of causing division in the body of Christ —either by tale bearing, which separates others, or by pride and self-righteousness, which separates you from the body—confess this as sin and turn from it so that your faith may grow. Take your proper place in the Body, whether it is small or great, and help others to do the same.

Accept the blood of Christ for the cleansing of your sins, and then accept by faith, the body of Christ for the healing of your body. It is yours. Jesus bought it for you the day He bought your salvation upon the cross. Discern now the body of the Lord and you, too, shall enjoy the blessing of healing for your body. Satan cannot legally afflict you with that for which Christ has already suffered in your place.

Many are sick today who once experienced marvelous

healings. Some even complain of the same sickness from which they were so gloriously delivered. When Jesus was here on earth He indicated that this would be the case. This does not mean that it is not God's will for these people to be well, or that they cannot be permanently healed. To one whom Christ had healed, He warned, Sin no more, lest a worse thing come unto thee (John 5:14).

God does not heal a person in order to give him more strength to continue in sin. Sickness has returned to many because of their own carelessness and disobedience to God. (This matter will be dealt with more fully in Chapter 12—"Keeping Your Healing." If you have been unable to keep your healing, be sure to read this chapter. You need not be discouraged, for you, too, can have deliverance.)

Proper health care is a must

Much sickness is caused by improper care of the body. The laws of nature are God's laws for physical health and cannot be broken without punishment in the form of sickness or infirmity. Divine healing was never intended to take the place of proper care of the body such as rest, exercise, eating the right foods, and avoiding habits that weaken the body.

God commanded His people to rest one day out of every seven days. While we are no longer under legal bondage to keep the Sabbath, which was a shadow of a better rest to come (see Hebrews 4:9), Jesus himself declared that the Sabbath was made for man, and not man for the Sabbath (Mark 2:27). One day's rest out of seven has been proven essential for good health. Those who cannot find time to rest, who keep themselves too busy with the cares of life to attend worship in the house of God, make themselves susceptible to the inroads of disease. Neither can they gain faith to receive healing, for faith cometh by hearing, and hearing by the word of God (Romans 10:17). Healing is available to all God's people, but only through faith, and faith cannot come in any other way but by hearing and obeying the Word of God. Many desire prayer for their bodies, but insist they cannot attend services to receive instruction about healing from the Word of God. They work every day, including Sunday and many of these people suffer from nervous disorders. The increasing number of nervous disorders and mental and physical breakdowns due to fatigue can be traced directly to an increasing lack of concern for the command of God: Six days shalt thou labor, and do all thy work: but the seventh day is the Sabbath of the Lord thy God: in it thou shalt not do any work (Exodus 20:9–10).

The medical profession defines many diseases as deficiency diseases, meaning that they are caused by a lack of essential elements in the diet. Christians would do well to consider the value of the various foods God has placed in the world and choose a diet that will keep their bodies strong and well. This is not a matter of the soul's salvation, but is vitally important to the body's health.

Overeating

Jesus said, Man shall not live by bread alone. The eternal values of the kingdom of God are far greater than the present enjoyment of pleasant food and drink. We are advised that everyone that striveth for the mastery is temperate in all things (1 Corinthians 9:25). Overeating is the direct cause of some sicknesses and is a contributing factor in many others. The work of all the organs of the body such as the liver, stomach, and heart, are so increased by overeating as to make it impossible for them to carry on their normal duties, and sicknesses result, ranging from gout to stomach and heart trouble. Even deficiency diseases are frequently prevalent among those who overeat because they choose their foods on the basis of taste appeal rather than the body's needs. Too many rich, sweet foods, too much meat, or too many starchy foods can make the body fat, overburden the heart and digestive system and, at the same time, fail to provide the nutrients needed for good health. Many people who come requesting prayer for their bodies would never have needed to come had they taken a little more care in choosing a proper diet. And they would benefit very little from an instant, miraculous healing. They would immediately start the process over again of tearing down their health through the same disobedience to the laws of nature, which originally caused their sickness.

Bad habits

Then there are those who injure their bodies through weakening habits. It may seem unnecessary to mention such things as the use of liquor, narcotics, and tobacco, but there are many who are still in bondage to one or all of these habits. It is a well-known fact, substantiated by the best medical authorities, as well as athletes, coaches, and others interested in building strong bodies, that all these habits are injurious to the body. Many diseases, especially of the heart and liver are directly traceable to the use of these drugs. First Corinthians 3:17 declares, If any man defile the temple of God, him shall God destroy; for the temple of God is holy, which temple ye are. It seems almost inconceivable, in light of this verse that any should expect healing from God while defiling their bodies with these recognized poisons. If you are in bondage to any of these habits, it is time to set your body free. When you attempt to lay it aside, you will, no doubt, soon realize what a hold it had on your body. But God said, If the Son therefore shall make you free, ye shall be free indeed (John 8:36). When you recognize this filthy habit as a bondage and look to God for grace, He will set you free! Then, when you have been delivered from the disease through the power of God, the cause of the disease will also be gone, and you can stay well.

God chose to make His abode in human bodies, as evidenced by many scriptures, including 1 Corinthians 3:17, quoted above, and also 1 Corinthians 6:19, What?

know ye not that your body is the temple of the Holy Ghost? Every Christian is a caretaker of His temple. This is a sacred trust and responsibility, and God is not glorified by our abuse of our bodies.

Carelessly exposing the body to extreme temperatures or germs of contagious diseases comes under the heading of "tempting God" and may readily bring on sickness. If exposure to these dangers is necessary, we can claim God's protection. As long as we walk by faith we need not be in bondage to fear.

CHAPTER 5
THE ABSOLUTE NECESSITY OF FAITH

Thy faith hath made thee whole (Mark 5:34).

According to your faith be it unto you (Matthew 9:29).

As thou hast believed, so be it unto thee (Matthew 8:13).

He that wavereth is like a wave of the sea driven with the wind and tossed. Let not that man think that he shall receive anything of the Lord (James 1:6–7).

According to Mark 5:24–34, a certain woman had an issue of blood for twelve years. She had suffered many things of many physicians and spent all that she had. But instead of getting better, she rather grew worse. Finally, hearing of Jesus, she sought Him and touched His garment and was made whole. What made this woman whole? Many will say, "Christ." In a sense, that is right, for without touching Him she could never have been healed. But after she was healed, Christ himself said, Daughter, thy faith hath made thee whole (verse 34). According to Jesus' own words, it was her faith that made her whole. She never would have overcome the difficulties in her path, which seemingly made it impossible for her to touch Him, had she not had faith.

At another time, two blind men came to Jesus for healing. He touched their eyes and they were opened.

What was it that opened the blind eyes? After Jesus touched them, He declared, According to your faith be it unto you (Matthew 9:29). In reality, it was their faith, in cooperation with the power of God through Jesus Christ that brought about their healing.

Jesus said to the centurion, As thou hast believed, so be it done unto thee (Matthew 8:13).

In reading the New Testament accounts of healing in the ministry of Jesus and His early followers, we may find many statements such as these. All the promises of God are conditioned upon faith. There is no other way to receive anything from God. James states this fact in the clearest possible language. Let him ask in faith, nothing wavering. For he that wavereth is like a wave of the sea driven with the wind and tossed...let not that man think that he shall receive any thing of the Lord (James 1:6,7). Faith is an absolute necessity if one is to receive anything from God.

Gifts of healing + faith = healing

Many today have a mistaken idea that, since many are exercising the gifts of healing and miracles, all they need to do is attend one of their meetings and they will be healed, without faith on their part. They think that the gift of healing will take the place of their own faith in God. This is not scriptural! The gift of healing will not take the place of your own faith in God.

There is no doubt that Christ exercised all the gifts of the Spirit, including healings and miracles. Yet when He went to Nazareth, He could there do no mighty work, save that he laid his hands upon a few sick folk, and healed them (Mark 6:5). And he did not many mighty works there because of their unbelief (Matthew 13:58).

The gifts of healing possessed by the Lord himself did not bring healing to others independent of their faith. Neither will the gift of healing exercised by men of God today bring healing to you unless you have faith.

Paul met a certain man at Lystra, impotent in his feet. Paul said to the man with a loud voice, Stand upright on thy feet (Acts 14:10). The man was healed immediately and leaped and walked! Notice that, according to verse 9, before Paul commanded him to stand upon his feet, he perceived that he had faith to be healed. Although Paul exercised the gifts of healing and miracles, he recognized that they were insufficient, in themselves, to bring about the desired result. Faith on the part of the suffering person was necessary to bring about healing.

When Christ healed the woman the of Mark 5:25, He did not say "Daughter, my gift hath made thee whole," but rather, "Thy faith hath made thee whole." Paul didn't say to the impotent man, "All right, fellow, get a card and get in line. I've got the gift of healing." Rather, Paul looked the situation over and discerned that the man had faith to be healed!

It is a marvelous privilege today to be able to attend meeting where God's anointed men are bringing deliverance in the name of Jesus! But this, in itself, is not enough. If Christ himself were conducting the meetings and laying His hands upon the sick today, He would, no doubt, say to them as in the days of old, "Thy faith hath made thee whole!"

Borrowed faith

Many people confess that they do not have much faith and wonder if it is possible for them to be healed through some other person's faith. Many have said to me, "I do not have any faith, but can't I be healed through your faith?"

James 5:16 says, The effectual fervent prayer of a righteous man availeth much. But God's guarantee is to those who themselves have faith! If a person received healing without having faith, it certainly would be the exception, and not the rule laid down in His Word.

You might be healed through another's faith, but how would you keep that healing? Faith is necessary not only to receive healing, but also to retain it, for Satan is not easily defeated. Almost without exception, when a person has been healed, Satan will immediately attack him, in an attempt to snatch from him the gift that God has given. Thus, if your healing depended upon another's faith, Satan would only have to wait until the other person was not present to find you utterly defenseless and take your healing from you. This is why many suffer today from diseases they were once healed of.

Do not be discouraged if your faith is low. The next chapter is written with you in mind. It will build your faith, if you follow its instructions. Read it prayerfully and obediently. As you do, the flame of your faith will burn brighter and brighter.

CHAPTER 6
HAVE THE FAITH THE GOD GIVES

In the preceding chapter we found that faith is an absolute requirement for healing. There are thousands of promises in God's Word, and every one is conditioned upon faith. Faith that you can have! Faith that God gives!

Christ, on His way to Bethany one day, cursed a fig tree because it produced no fruit (see Mark 11:12). He declared that no man would eat fruit of that tree thereafter. A mighty miracle had been performed, although it was not immediately apparent. Faith had been exercised. The following morning, the disciples again saw the fig tree, but it was dried up at the roots. Peter expressed his amazement at finding that the tree was withered away. Jesus answered him, Have faith in God. For verily I say unto you, That whosoever shall say unto this mountain, Be thou removed, and be thou cast into the sea; and shall not doubt in his heart...he shall have whatsoever he saith (Mark 11:22–23). It is clear that others can have the same faith Jesus exercised.

We can have the faith of God, literally, the faith that

God gives!

The price of faith

God does give faith. God gives faith to every person who wants it badly enough to pay the price required. That price is obedience, godliness, and holiness, following in the footsteps of Jesus, living free from condemnation, and walking in the full light of the Scriptures.

The Apostle John declares, If our heart condemn us not, then [and then only] have we confidence toward God (1 John 3:21). Faith and confidence is the same thing. Webster's dictionary defines faith as "complete confidence in a person." Surely no one can merit our complete confidence more fully than God!

Faith is not a mysterious, thrilling feeling going up and down one's spine. Faith is a common, everyday thing, which is evidenced in all the activities of daily life. You write a letter, go to the post office, buy a tiny stamp, place it on the comer of the envelope, and drop the letter into a mailbox slot - having complete confidence that the person to whom you addressed the letter will receive it within a few days. You do not have a sudden, overwhelming feeling that your friend will receive the letter. It just doesn't enter your mind to doubt that he will receive the letter.

Some people have more faith in Uncle Sam than in Jesus. Yet there is no reason to doubt the promises of God, if we have carried out our part.

If the letter wasn't placed in the post office, or if the stamp was left off, there might be reason to doubt that our friend will receive the letter. Likewise, if we refuse or neglect to do our part in getting our petitions to God, there is no reason to expect an answer from Him. But if we do our part, God absolutely guarantees to do His part - healing is ours!

Now that we know what we are trying to obtain, let us consider the scriptural methods of obtaining it. No matter how trustworthy an acquaintance may be, we can never feel entirely sure that he merits complete confidence until we are thoroughly acquainted with him. This is the reason many people fail to trust God. We become acquainted with God by walking with Him day by day, and by reading His Word. Faith cometh by hearing, and hearing by the word of God (Romans 10:17). Read God's Word. Read it as you would a letter from a trusted friend. Consider it the final authority. Turn resolutely away from books and conversations, which question the truth of God's Word.

Jesus accused a religious group in His day of making the word of God of none effect through your traditions (Mark 7:13), and of teaching for doctrines the commandments of men (Mark 7:7). Many preachers today set at naught the promises of God, basing their teaching on the things they have observed around them, rather than on the Word of God. Faith can only be built upon the power and success of the Word of God, never upon our own or another's weaknesses and failures.

Then faith, having been planted in the heart through the Word, must be watered and nourished through a genuine love for God. Perfect love casteth out fear (1 John 4:18). Fear is the direct opposite of faith. It is the murderer of faith. There is no fear in love. You cannot have faith if you do not love God. You can hope He will heal. You may say, "I know He is able." But you cannot have faith.

Obey God's Commandments

If you love God, you will keep His commandments (see John 14:15,21,23). Failure to keep His commandments is the reason many fail to have faith. Faith...worketh by love (Galatians 5:6). Love is manifested by obedience. Disobedience to the known will of God indicates a lack of faith and love. If we love God, we will be concerned about knowing and doing His will.

I believe the greatest hindrance to faith today is disobedience. John says, Beloved, if our heart condemn us not, then have we confidence toward God. And whatsoever we ask, we receive of him, because we keep his commandments, and do those things that are pleasing in his sight (1 John 3:21–22).

Real faith—living, vital faith—is impossible to people who are not in harmony with the personality and the Spirit of God, because they are living in disobedience to God's commandments.

Many people today who profess to be Christians are living under constant condemnation for sin and disobedience to the known will and Word of God. Such a person can never have real faith until he has first repented of his sins and turned his back upon them. For only then will that condemnation leave. Only then can he have a clear conscience toward God, which brings perfect confidence, or faith.

Receive the Holy Ghost

The confidence of some may be destroyed because of living in the condemnation that light—the light of the scriptures concerning the baptism of the Holy Ghost—has come into the world, and they have not walked in that light. They know that they should have this glorious experience, but they have not met the conditions to receive it.

Have ye received the Holy Ghost since ye believed? (Acts 19:2). Surely this cannot be termed an unfair question to Christians. Paul asked this question of a group of twelve believers at Ephesus. Every Christian should have this experience, not only because God commanded it (and that should be reason enough), but also because the Christian needs this power to work and witness for his Lord.

In the New Testament church, every member was filled with the Holy Ghost. All Christian individuals and groups spoken of in the New Testament were baptized with the Holy Ghost, as a separate and different experience from conversion, and coming after conversion. The disciples of

Jesus were all saved, inasmuch as Christ had commissioned them to preach the gospel and to heal the sick, and had been given power and authority over devils (see Luke 9:1–2). Their names were written in heaven (see Luke 10:20), an evident sign that they were saved. Yet Jesus commanded them that they should not depart from Jerusalem, but wait for the promise of the Father, which, saith he, ye have heard of me. For John truly baptized with water; but ye shall be baptized with the Holy Ghost not many days hence (Acts 1:4–5).

And, behold, I send the promise of the Father upon you: but tarry ye in the city of Jerusalem, UNTIL ye be endued with power from on high (Luke 24:49). This is not just a commandment to a few people in days gone by, but it is for Christians everywhere today. While preaching his first Holy Ghost sermon after receiving the Holy Spirit, Peter said, Repent, and be baptized every one of you in the name of Jesus Christ for the remission of sins, and ye shall receive the gift of the Holy Ghost. For the promise is unto you, and to your children, and to all that are afar off, even as many as the Lord our God shall call (Acts 2:38–39).

Many consider the baptism of the Holy Ghost to be a mere privilege instead of a direct command. However, it is a command, for Paul said, Be not drunk with wine, wherein is excess; but be filled with the Spirit (Ephesians 5:18). Since this is a command, one must be obedient to God's command. Those who have come into the light of God's truth are expected to walk in that light, and failure to do so brings condemnation. And this is the condemnation, that light is come into the world, and men loved darkness rather than light, because their deeds were evil (John 3:19). Many people today are, more or less, living under condemnation because they have not made a consecration of full obedience that they might receive this glorious experience, the baptism of the Holy Ghost.

Acts 5:32 makes it clear that those who are obedient have received the Holy Ghost. And we are witnesses of these things; and so is also the Holy Ghost, whom God hath given to them that obey him. It is evident from this verse that, if you have not been filled with the Holy Ghost, you have not yet been fully obedient. And if you haven't been obedient, then you have been disobedient. Disobedience is sin...sin brings condemnation... condemnation destroys faith.

Abide in Christ

If ye abide in me, and my words abide in you, ye shall ask what ye will, and it shall be done unto you (John 15:7). One must abide in Christ to be in a position to exercise real faith before he can receive the faith that God gives. God does not give faith to people who do not abide in Him. If He did, anyone - even drunkards, harlots, thieves, murderers, and the enemies of the kingdom of God - would be able to have and exercise faith and receive from God anything they asked. But since the blessings of God are for those who serve Him and put Him first in their lives, one must abide in Christ before faith can actually be exercised.

Let's look in God's Word for the definition of abiding in Christ. He that saith he abideth in him ought himself also so to walk, even as he walked (1 John 2:6). In this verse, it is quite clear that, if we profess to abide in Christ, we should be walking as He walked. Friend, if you are not walking as Christ walked, you are not abiding in Him, and it's no wonder you have no faith! You can never be on real faith ground until you begin to abide in Christ and walk as He walked. This is not only possible, but it is God's command.

Christ also suffered for us, leaving us an example, that we should follow his steps: Who did no sin (1 Peter 2:21–22). Christ did not live in habitual sin. He did not make excuses for sin. He resisted the devil and temptation although He was in all points tempted like as we are, yet without sin (Hebrews 4:15). He is our example. And He stands ready to help us walk as He walked - in His steps.

Whosoever abideth in him sinneth not (1 John 3:6).

I am aware that this teaching is contrary to much of today's religious teaching. I'm also aware that multitudes who claim to be children of God and believe in divine healing have been prayed for again and again, without being able to exercise faith for healing. This matter is of sufficient importance to make it worthwhile to face facts, regardless of opinions. There is a reason why these people continue in their sicknesses, pains, and diseases, and cannot receive healing for their sick bodies. It is not because God is a respecter of persons. Often it is because the afflicted person has not paid the price of faith, which is obedience and holiness.

Live a holy life

Hope is available to people without holiness, but faith is not! If people without holiness could have faith, they could have anything they desire from God, for God's guarantee to those who have faith is, Whatsoever ye shall ask in prayer, believing, ye shall receive (Matthew 21:22). And God also said, Follow peace ... and holiness, without which no man shall see the Lord (Hebrews 12:14).

It is a common teaching today that everyone sins all the time, that it is impossible to live above sin, and that, as long as we are is in this world, we must partake of a certain number of the sins of this life. Those who teach this doctrine quote numerous scriptures that pertain only to the unregenerate man who has never had a salvation experience. But God says, Be ye holy; for I am holy (1 Peter 1:16).

Paul says, Awake to righteousness, and sin not; for some have not the knowledge of God: I speak this to your shame (1 Corinthians 15:34).

According to this verse, those who find excuses for their habitual sin do not have the knowledge of God. What a shame! It is evident that such professed Christians do not read their Bibles.

After Jesus had healed a man, He found him in the temple and said to him, Behold, thou art made whole: sin no more, lest a worse thing come upon thee (John 5:14).

To the woman of Samaria, Christ said, Go, and sin no more (John 8:11).

My little children, these things write I unto you, that ye sin not (1 John 2:1).

Paul settled the sin question in Romans 6:1–2 when he said, What shall we say then? Shall we continue, in sin, that grace may abound? God forbid!

When people again share the attitude of Christ concerning the sin question and begin to abide in God, multitudes will again be healed and books like this will be unnecessary. But until people are enlightened and learn the truth, books like this must be written.

Numerous people today are asking the question, "Why wasn't I healed?" The answer is simple: because of no faith, or insufficient faith. There is more than one reason for lack of faith, but the main reason is lack of holiness. Another outstanding reason is the common neglect of Bible study. No wonder there is a lack of faith in the hearts of so many today.

God Himself has established the price of faith. Love God. Read His Word. Obey His commands. Believe His promises.

To some, this may seem like an impossible price, but God has enabled man to pay it. The same Christ who saves from sin will keep those who desire to be kept by His mighty power. The Lord is faithful, who shall stablish you, and keep you from evil (2 Thessalonians 3:3).

Now unto him that is able to keep you from falling, and to present you faultless before the presence of his glory with exceeding joy (Jude 24).

God not only commands that we abide in Him, but He makes it possible by giving us power to resist the devil in temptation. There hath no temptation taken you but such as is common to man: But God is faithful, who will not suffer you to be tempted above that ye are able; but will with the temptation also make a way to escape, that ye may be able to bear it (1 Corinthians 10:13).

I have found that those who have a real desire to please God, those who read their Bibles and pray, are attaining holiness. It is these same people who are shouting the victory over sickness, disease, and the power of the enemy. God has given them faith.

Faith—a gift and fruit of the Spirit

Faith is listed as one of the nine gifts of the Spirit (see 1 Corinthians 12:9). Time and space will not permit us to dwell at length upon faith as one of the nine gifts. Suffice it to say that the faith mentioned here is a gift of the Spirit, given by the Spirit. The Church is admonished in verse 31 to covet earnestly the best gifts.

All Christians have a certain amount of faith. It is impossible even to be saved without it. At the moment of salvation, faith begins to grow like a fruit, for faith is a fruit of the Spirit as well as a spiritual gift (see Galatians 5:22). As some trees in an orchard produce very little fruit, or fruit of poor quality, so some Christians seem to produce very little fruit of the Spirit. Fruit must first bud, then grow and develop. For proper development of the fruit of faith, it must be properly nourished like the fruit in the orchard. Since faith cometh by hearing the Word of God, the Christian should read the Word of God often. Memorize many of the promises of God that pertain to healing and stand upon them. Quote them again and again. In this way, faith will grow.

Faith must be built upon the Word of God and only upon the Word of God. The experiences and testimonies of others merely bring hope, not faith. Faith cannot be built merely upon the experiences of others. It cannot be built upon one's feelings or upon that which has been seen. Seeing the mighty power of God bring healing to others will cause hope to spring up in the heart, but this is not faith. It is helpful to faith, but cannot take the place of faith - Faith cometh by hearing, and hearing by the word of God (Romans 10:17). Base your faith exclusively upon the Word of God. Don't talk in terms of what you may or may not feel. People who gauge their healing by their feelings never credit anything to God's Word. The person who accepts God's Word for his own case, whether the results are visible and "feelable" or not, will soon see and feel the results, for this is the faith that God gives. Real faith is simply taking God at His Word. The more of God's Word you have hidden in your heart, the easier it is to believe and exercise faith in that Word.

There are many hindrances to faith, and the next chapter deals with this subject. Read it carefully and prayerfully and follow the instructions, and the God who never fails will surely reward your obedience with a real, vital, and living faith—the faith that God gives! This kind of faith can claim God's guarantee of healing which cannot fail.

CHAPTER 7
HINDRANCES TO FAITH

Faith is taking God at His Word.

It is easy to see that sin would prevent one from having faith to accept healing since God's Word does not promise healing to the sinner. We know that God heareth not sinners (John 9:31). God's promise to sinners is that He will forgive their sins when they repent and will judge their sins if they do not repent.

God's promises to answer prayer and bring healing are for His obedient children. If ye abide in me, and my words abide in you, ye shall ask what ye will, and it shall be done unto you (John 15:7). Abiding in Christ guarantees that your prayers will be answered.

Failure to abide in Christ should be first on any list of hindrances to faith, for it nullifies God's guarantee.

Abiding in Christ is not accomplished through church

membership or being kind to your neighbors. It is not accomplished through singing in the choir, teaching a Sunday school class, preaching, or praying. To abide in Christ, you must live in and by the Word of God and be in joyful fellowship with God. There is no condemnation to them which are in Christ Jesus (Romans 8:1).

Many ask amiss

Some people ask of God and receive. Others ask in the same words and receive nothing. This is not a matter of chance or respect of persons, but of faith. Ye ask and receive not, because ye ask amiss, that ye may consume it upon your lusts (James 4:3). This kind of asking can never be done in faith. There may be a desire to be well and even a hope that "it may work," but there cannot be faith, for in this type of asking there is no promise upon which faith can be based. Some desire healing in order to better carry on their sinful pursuits. A society lady wanted healing for her drawn and crippled hands so she could deal the playing cards more gracefully. Simon the sorcerer desired to be able to impart the Holy Ghost by the laying on of hands so that he might turn this gift to his own financial profit (see Acts 8). God does not give faith to such people. Used indiscriminately, by those who are governed by their own lust, it can even be dangerous. For this reason, it is given only to those who abide in Christ and in whom His words abide. Only these can be trusted to use such a mighty power.

Condemnation

Those who abide in Christ are not condemned. If our heart condemn us not, then have we confidence toward God. And whatsoever we ask, we receive of him, because we keep his commandments, and do those things that are pleasing in his sight (1 John 3:21–22). This is God's formula for faith. Until you have met this condition, you cannot have faith. You may be persuaded that God is able to heal you, but you can only hope that He will, for He has not promised to do it while you live in sin, under condemnation.

I may know a millionaire who could easily give me a thousand dollars. I know he could do it. He may have given one of my friends a thousand dollars. I may have even seen the check. I may need it very badly and hope fervently that he will somehow decide to give me a thousand dollars. But I have no real reason to believe that he will unless he says that he will.

God's power is sufficient to heal everybody, as well as to save them. But His promise is to heal those who keep His commandments and walk in His statutes, those who believe that all of His words are truth.

Condemnation is, no doubt, the greatest hindrance to faith. Let's consider a few of the things that bring condemnation to Christians and hinder their faith. Anything that is of a disobedient, ungodly, unholy nature is a hindrance to faith.

Peter exhorts husbands and wives regarding their relationship: Likewise, ye wives, be in subjection to your husbands; that, if any obey not the word, they also may without the word be won by the conversation of the wives; Likewise, ye husbands, dwell with them according to knowledge, giving honor unto the wife, as unto the weaker vessel, and as being heirs together of the grace of life; that your prayers be not hindered (1 Peter 3:1,7).

The faith of many is hindered because of unscriptural relationships in the home. But unscriptural attitudes toward our fellowman outside the home can also be a great hindrance to faith. What things soever ye desire, when ye pray, believe that ye receive them, and ye shall have them. And when ye stand praying, forgive, if ye have ought against any (Mark 11:24–25). An unforgiving spirit hinders faith.

The tithe ... is the LORD'S (Leviticus 27:30).

Many professed Christians live under constant

condemnation because they refuse to give God His tithe. They know that the Bible teaches consistent tithing and that a tenth of their increase should be given to God for the support of the ministry. Yet great numbers of church people refuse to walk in the light of God's Word. Many of these so-called "saints" help to make up our healing lines. God calls them thieves (see Malachi 3:8). If you have been robbing God, do not expect Him to heal you until you have first asked His pardon and become a tither. True, the law required tithing, but the tithe is older than the law. And God's promises are still true. Bring ye all the tithes into the storehouse, that there may be meat in mine house, and prove me now herewith, saith the LORD of hosts, if I will not open you the windows of heaven, and pour you out a blessing, that there shall not be room enough to receive it (Malachi 3:10).

Another hindrance to faith is found in James 5:16. Confess your faults one to another, and pray one for another, that ye may be healed. Many people are quick to see the faults of others, but are seemingly blind to faults of their own. With this spirit, one can hardly expect to have faith to trust God for healing.

Few people claim to be perfect, yet when confronted with the necessity of confessing faults in order to receive healing, they are still not willing to confess. While many receive immediate healing in healing lines, others pass through many healing lines and yet they are not healed. According to James 5:14, these people need to call in the elders of the church for help. With much heart-searching and prayer, they need to search their lives to find the reason why healing has been withheld. Then, when the light of God has revealed the problem, they should confess that fault to those who are praying with them and pray together that the fault may be overcome. Then, in answer to the united prayers of the afflicted person and the elders who have been called in to help, Satan can be driven from the field, and a double victory can be won. The bondage of both sin and sickness will be broken.

Those who hear such confession must remember that, in the cause of Christian brotherhood, they are under obligation to speak of the faults to no one except God.

Any unwillingness to confess faults usually indicates an unwillingness to forsake them, or a lack of confidence in the power of God to bring deliverance. This is one of the greatest hindrances to faith.

A form of godliness

We are warned in God's Word that in the last days there shall be those in the world having a form of godliness, but denying the power thereof (2 Timothy 3:5). Surely this does not apply to those who make no profession of godliness, but to churches and ministers who make loud professions of godliness, but deny that there is any supernatural power in operation in the work today. Instead of conversion by means of a new birth, they advise good resolutions, church membership, or baptism. None of these things can change the heart.

One such religious man came to recognize the futility of his own doctrine and sincerely sought God's way. To him, Jesus said, Ye must be born again (John 3:7). Some who call themselves "Fundamentalists" accept this much of the miracle-working power of God, but no more. They agree with Mark 16:16, He that believeth and is baptized shall be saved, but they deny the power of verses 17 and 18, These signs shall follow them that believe; In my name shall they cast out devils; they shall speak with new tongues; They shall take up serpents; and if they drink any deadly thing, it shall not hurt them; they shall lay hands on the sick, and they shall recover.

They gather together in churches and sing hymns, preach sermons, pray beautiful prayers, and some even baptize with water and take the Lord's Supper. They have all the outward forms of godliness and are recognized by the world and government as "the Church." But they absolutely deny the power Jesus promised to leave with the godly. In the same verse with the warning quoted at the beginning of this thought, God tells us clearly what to do if we are associated with such a group of people—from such turn away (2 Timothy 3:5).

Many fail to receive healing because they have not heeded this warning. The spark of faith has begun to glow in their hearts, but instead of assembling themselves together with others of like precious faith who will encourage and guide them into an ever greater faith, they insist on remaining in the company of those who not only do not believe in the miracle-working power of God, but who openly deny that there is any such power.

Your personal faith has as good a chance of surviving in such circumstances as a coal of fire in a tub of ice water. God has not called you to remain in such an environment. It is very well to tell them of what you have found in God's Word. If they also believe, you have won a friend in Christ. But if they will not believe, then the Word of God clearly says to turn away from them. They have turned away their ears from the truth and will turn you away from the truth also, if you continue in their company.

Search the scriptures. Build your faith upon the Word of God and then get into a church, which has done the same. Many, many people are hindered from receiving healing faith because they have failed to heed this important instruction from God's Word.

God has guaranteed to heal those who ask in faith, without wavering. The only way that Satan can prevent you from receiving the healing God has promised you is to keep you from asking in faith. This he accomplishes by tricking you into allowing hindrances to remain in your life. Examine your heart and life today. Get rid of the hindrances. Then you can come to God with no condemnation. If our heart condemn us not, then have we confidence toward God. And whatsoever we ask, we receive of him (1 John 3:21–22).

One of the most prevalent hindrances to faith is found in the common misconceptions regarding the teachings of

God's Word, which will be discussed in the next chapter. These are largely due to erroneous teaching by those who do not have the power of God in their own lives. They make excuses for themselves by adjusting the teaching of Scripture to their own thinking. Although they may be very learned in the things of this world, from God's standpoint they are unlearned and unstable and wrest the Scriptures...to their own destruction.

CHAPTER 8
MISCONCEPTIONS REGARDING HEALING

Many born-again Christians who are living sincerely and wholeheartedly for God remain afflicted after prayer for healing. This may be due to a misconception regarding the teachings of God's Word. Perhaps they have not been able to understand that God promises healing to all who ask in faith. They do not realize the extent of God's great guarantee to heal and, because of this misconception, they have asked with wavering faith.

Unwavering faith

God says, Let him ask in faith, nothing wavering. For he that wavereth is like a wave of the sea driven with the wind and tossed. For let not that man think that he shall receive any thing of the Lord (James 1:6–7).

Often these people come for prayer thinking that they DO believe and will not waver in faith. But when it's put to the test, they find that their faith wavers. They say, "I really thought I was going to be healed this time, but I just can't seem to have enough faith."

These people really do have faith. But their faith wavers because of misconceptions regarding the Word of God which have commonly been taught as doctrines, but which really cannot be proven by the Word of God. These are traditions of men which make the word of God of none effect (Mark 7:13) to the person who heeds them.

Jesus says of those who teach in this way, In vain do they worship me, teaching for doctrines the commandments of men (Mark 7:7, Matthew 15:9).

God has guaranteed healing to His people. But some who profess to be His ministers have told the people that He didn't mean what He said!

Suffering for God's glory

Another prominent misconception is that some cannot be healed because they are suffering for the glory of God. This teaching is based on two misinterpreted incidents in the ministry of Christ.

When Jesus was told that Lazarus was sick, He replied, This sickness is not unto death, but for the glory of God, that the Son of God might be glorified thereby (John 11:4).

When Jesus finally came to Bethany and was met by the sisters of Lazarus, He certainly was not met with praise. They were not glorifying God or His Son. But the Son of God was glorified when Lazarus came forth from the tomb (see verse 44).

In another case, some of Jesus' disciples questioned Him concerning a man who was born blind. They wondered whether the man had sinned or his parents. (This is an example of the mistaken attitude of that time regarding the relation between sin and sickness.) Jesus answered, Neither hath this man sinned, nor his parents: but that the works of God should be made manifest in him (John 9:3).

This does not infer that neither this man nor his parents had ever committed a sin, for we are told, All have sinned, and come short of the glory of God (Romans 3:23). Rather, this blindness, which was unusual, was not a direct punishment for unusual sin.

But if this man was blind for God's glory, then Jesus was working against the glory of God, for He gave sight that day to the man. This man's blindness was not, in itself, a glory to God. But rather, his blindness was an occasion for the works of God to be made manifest in him. When people saw this man, blind from birth, suddenly receive his sight, God was glorified.

If you are suffering for God's glory, then let God be glorified NOW by accepting healing from Him. Be a witness to everyone around you of the mighty power of God that brings deliverance to all who trust in Him!

Not once in His entire earthly ministry did Jesus ever command a person to be sick. However, He commanded many to be well and healed them with His Word. Not once did a sick person come to Him, asking to be healed, and receive the answer, "It is God's will for you to remain sick for His glory."

Jesus Christ the same yesterday, and to day, and for ever (Hebrews 13:8). Then it is inconceivable that, while He was here on earth, He glorified the Father by healing all manner of sickness and all manner of disease among the people (Matthew 4:23), but now, having gone back to the Father, He is glorified by people remaining patient in affliction, declaring that it is evidence of His love. It is no wonder that sinners are not interested in sharing in such love!

Nowhere in the Word of God is sickness declared to be an evidence of God's favor. Rather, it is the penalty for sin (see Deuteronomy 28:22–28,61). The reward of obedience is health and healing (see Exodus 15:26).

A glaring inconsistency in the "suffering for God's glory" theory is that, while these people do not come to God for healing, they seem to feel no qualms of conscience in doing all that human power can do to ease pain and restore health. If sickness is truly God's will for them, should they try to escape it?

Suppose I say to you, "I am laboring in this city for the glory of God. It is His will for me to labor here. But I will only stay until I can somehow find a way to get away from here. I'm leaving just as soon as I can earn, beg, or borrow the price of a bus ticket to take me away. I know it is God's will for me to be here, but He can only keep me here by making it impossible for me to leave!" People would be horrified and probably would accuse me of rebelling against God.

Nevertheless, some say they are suffering for God's glory and yet it is apparent that they will suffer only as long as it is impossible for them to make themselves well. Is this not inconsistent?

Sickness is not God's will

Sickness is the work of the devil. It is the will of God that His people prosper and be in health (3 John 2). Therefore, let us come to God without wavering, in full assurance that we are asking in His will.

And this is the confidence that we have in him, that, if we ask anything according to his will, he heareth us: And if we know that he hear us, whatsoever we ask, we know that we have the petitions that we desired of him (1 John 5:14–15).

Those who insist that some are sick because it is the will of God strengthen their position by quoting as examples a few cases in Scripture. They feel this is evidence that God has chosen some of His best servants to suffer affliction. At best, this is only circumstantial evidence and must be accepted "with reservations" in any court of law. Under careful examination, these cases break down like circumstantial evidence.

Strive for perfection

First, let's consider the matter of Job's boils. According to the testimony of God himself, Job was a perfect and upright man, in that he feareth God, and escheweth evil (Job 1:8). No divine or superhuman perfection is attributed to Job. Any Christian can and should be at least as perfect as was Job, for our opportunities, privileges, and power are far ahead of his. Jesus left us the commandment to be perfect, even as your Father which is in Heaven is perfect (Matthew 5:48). The Scriptures - which Job never had the privilege of reading because he lived before they were written - were given that the man of God may be perfect (2 Timothy 3:17).

No Christian who is satisfied with being anything less than perfect is in the will of God or in a position to seek healing. Though we may need to say with Paul, Not as though I had already attained, either were already perfect: but I follow after (Philippians 3:12), let us keep this goal constantly before us and earnestly "press toward the mark" at all times. Never make excuse for imperfections. Perfection is the goal.

God accounted Job as perfect because he sincerely feared God and eschewed (shunned, found no pleasure in doing) evil. However, a careful study of the Book of Job will reveal to the thoughtful reader enough reasons in Job himself for the trouble that came upon him. God does not submit His faithful and beloved followers to the tortures of Satan for no better reason than to merely prove a point to the devil. True enough, Job's faithfulness was proven, and Satan's boast proved empty, but a far greater issue than that was involved in the trial of Job. The Book of Job indicates that even a perfect man can be made better.

Fear is not faith

Note that, while Job was commended for his fear of God (see Job 1:8), this was not Job's only fear. When he was bereft of family and possessions, suffering in body, scorned by his wife, and misunderstood and accused by his friends, he cried out, The thing which I greatly feared is come upon me (Job 3:25).

Faith is our protection against sin and sickness, and it is our defense when these enemies lay hold on us. Satan saw it as a hedge around Job, which he could not penetrate. But fear, the opposite of faith, makes an opening in the hedge where Satan may enter. Job is not to be condemned for his attitude, for he did not have the Scriptures as we do today. His knowledge of God came only from oral tradition and an incomplete direct personal revelation of God. (It is generally recognized that Job was the first book of the Bible to be written.) Since faith cometh by hearing, and hearing by the Word of God, it is little wonder that Job failed to have sufficient faith to protect him from Satan's attack.

But having God's glorious promises so easily accessible, we should grasp them by faith and step forth into the glorious liberty available to the sons of God. As God's children, we need not grub in Job's ash heap, looking for an excuse to remain in bondage to the sickness and oppression of Satan.

God did not afflict Job. Satan...smote Job with sore boils (Job 2:7). But even this he could not do without God's permission.

A time of examination

In his desperation, Job examined his attitude toward God and, through the struggles of his soul, found a new relationship with God. True, he had feared God, striven to do right and avoid evil, but now, when his wife urged him to curse God and die (see Job 2:9), and his friends accused him of every kind of sin, calling them by name, Job discovered that only one thing remained a firm anchor in his fast-changing world. In his anguish he cried, Though he slay me, yet will I trust him (Job 13:15). God could not disregard such faith at that. Immediately, God began to work toward Job's deliverance. He revealed himself to Job in a glorious flash of splendor such as has seldom been equaled in His dealings with any one man. In light of this revelation, Job had a fine opportunity to compare his own righteousness with that of his Maker and found himself sadly lacking. He approached God then, not in a spirit of self-righteousness, but in true humility and repentance (see

Job 42:6) mixed with faith. He was even willing to pray for the deliverance of his accusers, and the Lord turned the captivity of Job, when he prayed for his friends (Job 42:10).

But the most beautiful part of the whole story is found in the concluding verses of the Book of Job. After Job had repented of his self-righteousness and lack of trust and had proven his humility and forgiveness by praying for his friends, God set him free from the captivity of Satan. Job was restored to all his former glory, with even more than he had at the beginning. He lived another 140 years, and there is no record that he ever had another boil to annoy him in all that time!

If you have been following Job's example, sitting in the ash heap bemoaning your fate and blaming it on God, you need to take another look at your example. Place your trust in God, as Job did, even though it may seem to lead only to death. Start searching the Scriptures, reading prayerfully, as though you had never heard the explanations men have added by their traditions. Look to God himself to find the cause of your sickness and, when you have found it, get rid of it. Then, like Job, you will be set free from bondage, for God is still the same today!

The enemies of the gospel of healing point to examples where true children of God were not healed. Because of that, they say there is no guarantee that God will heal all who meet His conditions. Seeing beforehand this attempt to discredit His work, the Lord has carefully shown us in His Word the reasons for the illnesses which persist for a time in the presence of the mighty miracle-working power of Christ and the first disciples with whom Christ worked, confirming the word with signs following (Mark 16:20).

Paul's ministry

God wrought special miracles in the ministry of Paul. Many whom he touched were healed, but even men and women who could not contact him personally were healed of diseases and delivered from evil spirits, when handkerchiefs or aprons were brought to them from Paul's body (see Acts 19:11–12).

We are told that his fellow soldier and companion in labor, Epaphroditus, became sick nigh unto death, while in the company of Paul. In fact, these are Paul's own words (see Philippians 2:27). However, Paul does not stop there. In the same verse, he declares that God had mercy on him, so that he was able to make the long journey from Rome to Philippi, despite the difficulty of such a journey in those times. This was a demonstration to the Philippians of the greatness of the power and love of God in his behalf. In verse 30, Paul explains the reason for the sickness. Because of the work of Christ he was nigh unto death, not regarding his life, to supply your lack of service toward me.

The gifts of healing do not guarantee an unlimited supply of strength and energy to the human body. It is possible, even in so worthy a work as carrying the gospel and praying for the sick, to tax the body beyond what God intended it to endure, with sickness as a result. But even here God shows His mercy. While a period of absolute rest or convalescence may be required, there is no need to be permanently defeated because of a nervous breakdown or other illness caused by overwork.

We are told that even Paul had his private physician—Luke—who traveled with him to watch after his health. It is true that Luke had been trained as a physician (see Colossians 4:14). However, there is just as much reason to declare that Jesus took Matthew with Him as His private tax collector as to assert that Luke was chosen to go with Paul because of his skill as a physician. There is no record in the Scriptures that Luke ever treated Paul or any other sick person in the capacity of a physician. Only one mention is made of him being a physician. As author of the Books of Luke and Acts, he records many miraculous hearings. It is noteworthy that every one of them is recorded as being one hundred percent miraculous. Never once is it recorded that Luke, or any other physician, applied any medical aid as a supplement to the miracle-working power of God. Being a physician, Luke was no doubt especially impressed when Christ and His Spirit filled disciples relieved diseases which physicians had tried in vain to heal. In fact, Luke records that a woman having an issue of blood twelve years, which had spent all her living upon physicians, neither could be healed of any, Came behind him, and touched the border of his garment: and immediately her issue of blood stanched (Luke 8:43–44).

The Great Physician

It is true that faithful physicians have relieved much human suffering. There are enough people in the world today who have never learned of the healing power of God to keep all the physicians busy and fully justify their existence in the world. But those who know the Great Physician should wait at His feet instead of in the overcrowded waiting rooms of earthly physicians. Here we can find the relief - full and free, without medicine or surgery - that our bodies may be well and strong for His glory. Surely He is worthy of every testimonial to His skill and faithfulness that His loving followers can give.

Many people have suffered for years while waiting to be treated by some of the famous physicians of our time. If only they would wait upon God and be as diligent to heed His directions as they are in carrying out the orders of earthly physicians, they would be healed.

Start today to examine yourself according to the Word of God. Find out what He says to do and do it. These treatments are not in the experimental stage. They are tried and proven—unconditionally guaranteed to be 100 percent effective, when used according to directions.

A thorn in the flesh

In an effort to prove that God denies healing to some, many quote 2 Corinthians 12:7–10; Lest I should be exalted above measure through the abundance of the revelations, there was given to me a thorn in the flesh, the messenger of Satan to buffet me, lest I should be exalted above measure. For this thing I besought the Lord thrice, that it might depart from me. And he said unto me, My grace is sufficient for thee: for my strength is made perfect in weakness...Therefore will I rather glory in my infirmities.

Whatever Paul's thorn may have been, God's grace was sufficient for him. The list of his achievements and sufferings in 2 Corinthians 11 would certainly be a sufficient test of grace. But to say that Paul's thorn was a physical defect would certainly require some backing beyond what is found in this passage of Scripture, for sickness is not mentioned. The strongest advocates of the idea that the thorn was a physical weakness dare not go further than to say, "It has been conjectured that Paul's thorn in the flesh was chronic ophthalmia" (Scofield Bible, page 1239).

In light of the glorious promises of healing given boldly in the Word of God, something stronger than a mere conjecture that Paul was sick should be required to cancel such strong promises.

The term, "thorn in the flesh," has so often been connected with sickness that it has come to have that meaning in the minds of many readers of this scripture. But let us examine its use in other scriptures to see if that was the thought of the writer.

In Numbers 33:55, the Israelites were warned, If ye will not drive out the inhabitants of the land from before you; then it shall come to pass, that those which ye let remain of them shall be pricks in your eyes, and thorns in your sides. This warning is repeated in Joshua 23:13 and Judges 2:3. Thus, the thorn refers not to something within the body but to annoyances from without, caused by people.

Paul speaks of his particular thorn as being the messenger of Satan to buffet me (2 Corinthians 12:7). The word buffet means "to strike as with the hand; to contend with."

In the list of the infirmities in which Paul chose to glory (see 2 Corinthians 11:23–33), there is no sickness or blindness mentioned, but rather persecutions. He does mention weariness and painfulness, but would not beatings, stonings, hunger, and cold be sufficient cause for weariness and painfulness?

After reviewing the list of Paul's sufferings and accomplishments, would it not require more faith in the miraculous to believe that he was carried through all these things while suffering from physical illness than to believe that he was kept in health by the power of God?

God is not a respecter of persons (see Colossians 3:25). His promises are yours! Let no man beguile you. Believe the Word of God and not the traditions that have been built around it.

As the flame of your faith burns brightly, no longer wavering, you can ask God for whatsoever He has promised and it shall be done unto you!

CHAPTER 9
WHY MANY DO NOT RECEIVE HEALING

If God still heals the sick today, why are so many good Christian people sick? Thousands of sick and suffering people in the world today would love to believe in divine healing, for it could mean deliverance from much suffering and sorrow. But they dare not rest their case in the hands of God and trust Him for deliverance until this question is answered.

Thousands more, who already believe in divine healing, ask almost the same question. They say, "Others are healed, so I know that God does heal today. But why do I not receive healing? Is God a respecter of persons?"

These questions cannot be ignored. God certainly has not ignored them, for the answers are in the Bible. There is no respect of persons with God (Romans 2:11).

If God's promises of healing apply to anyone, they apply to everyone.

Is any sick among you? let him call for the elders of the church; and let them pray over him, anointing him with oil in the name of the Lord: And the prayer of faith shall save the sick, and the Lord shall raise him up; and if he have committed sins, they shall be forgiven him (James 5:14–15).

As explained earlier, divine healing is not provided or promised for the enemies of Christ, or for those who continue to live in sin. The purpose here is to discover why Christian people fail to receive healing. If you desire to be healed and are not a Christian, you must first find healing for your soul. Repent of your sins and seek God with your whole heart. When you repent of your sins, believe in the Lord Jesus (not just some things about Him, but believe Him and trust Him and what He says in His Word), and confess Him with your mouth, then you will be saved (see Romans 10:9–10). When you are born again by the spirit of God and born into the family of God, you are eligible to ask in faith for any of His promised benefits.

The Christian and healing

If you are a Christian and still have not received healing, examine your life and attitudes in light of God's Word. God has not shown respect of persons in your case, for that is contrary to His divine nature. If you are still sick, there is a reason, and God's Word will reveal it to you if you will diligently seek His face. When you find the problem and correct it, God's healing touch will be yours. This is God's guarantee, and God cannot lie.

The reason that stands out above all others is lack of faith. You may say, "I have faith. I know God is able to heal me. But why does He not do it?"

Do you believe He will heal you...now?

You say, "I hope He will. I know God does heal today. I've been to Brother So-and-so's big meeting and seen hundreds healed. But when he laid his hands on me I didn't get healed."

What you have is not faith—it is hope. You hope to be healed. You have knowledge—you know God is able to heal and does heal. You believe what you have seen, but you do not have faith. Faith is believing what you have not seen, simply because God says it is so (see Hebrews 11:1). If you had faith, you would have already been healed.

A dear sister came to me with a deaf ear. She had been deaf in that ear for many years. She said, "I don't see why I don't get healed. I have as much faith as anyone. I have all the faith in the world." I carefully explained to her that if she had real, living faith to that extent, it would be impossible for her to remain deaf, because real faith works. Faith without works [faith that doesn't work] is dead (James 2:20). Real faith is guaranteed to bring results, for God is faithful to His promises. When she recognized that she was lacking in faith, she humbly asked God to forgive her for doubting Him and to help her unbelief. Immediately, her ear was unstopped.

This is a thoroughly scriptural approach to God in such a case. For Jesus once said to a man whose faith was weak, If thou canst believe, all things are possible to him that believeth (Mark 9:23). The man replied, with tears, Lord, I believe; help thou mine unbelief (verse 24). Immediately, Jesus helped his unbelief and his faith sprang up. He received the faith that God gives. And the thing he desired became not only a possibility, but also a reality - his son was delivered from Satan's power.

An honest confession of doubt, coupled with a sincere desire to learn how to believe, is far better than a loud profession of faith that does not work. It is hard to deceive yourself in this matter, and it is impossible to deceive God.

Real faith is not hoping that God will heal you, or

knowing that He is able to heal you. It is the joyful assurance that the work is as good as done, because God, who cannot lie, has promised—yes, even guaranteed—to heal you!

The fruit of the Spirit

Many fail to receive healing because they have been taught that sickness and physical suffering is God's way of bringing out the best in them, or developing the fruit of the Spirit in their lives. They believe that they must be patient in affliction and wait until it is God's time to heal them. They believe that, perhaps, God is working out patience and long-suffering in them. Or perhaps God is chastening them for some unknown sin.

It is true that sin opens the door for sickness to enter, but all God asks is that the sin be confessed and forsaken. God does not say, "Is any sick among you? Let him patiently wait until God has finished chastening him." But rather, Confess your faults one to another [now, today], and pray one for another, that ye may be healed. The promise is, The prayer of faith shall save the sick, and the Lord shall raise him up; and if he have committed sins, they shall be forgiven him (James 5:15–16).

God is not glorified when Christians continue in sickness or in the sin that caused it. But He is glorified when they are delivered from both.

Long-suffering (patience) is a fruit of the Spirit (see Galatians 5:22–23), not a "fruit of sickness and suffering." They result directly from yielding to the indwelling spirit of God. If, in some individuals, the fruit seems to result from sickness, it is because the sickness has driven them to give more attention to their relationship with the spirit of God than when they were well. Many people will agree that, in most cases, sickness results in less patience, not more.

If God (who never changes) uses this method to teach patience and long-suffering, surely, at some time in His earthly ministry, Jesus would have said to someone seeking deliverance, "Go thy way. Remain sick until you have learned patience. Then you may seek Me again, and perhaps I will heal you." But not once did He give such an answer. Not once did He command any person who was well to become sick, or anyone who was sick to remain so.

Sin and sickness are works of the devil

God certainly has not ordained that the fruit of the Spirit should be developed by the works of the devil. This is the work of the Spirit! Christ was manifested to destroy the works of the devil.

Some may say, "This may not be God's time to heal me. I will be faithful in my sickness and, in His own good time, God will heal me, should it be His will to do so."

This would be like a sinner saying, "This may not be God's time to save me. I will be faithful in my sin and disobedience and, if I am one God wills to save, surely He will save me in His own good time."

We know that it is the will of God to save everybody; for He is not willing that any should perish, but that all should come to repentance (2 Peter 3:9). However, none will escape except they repent, for Jesus said, Except ye repent, ye shall ALL likewise perish (Luke 13:5).

The moment a sinner repents, salvation is his. He need not wait and wonder if God will save him, for God says, If we confess our sins, he is faithful and just to forgive us our sins' and to cleanse us from all unrighteousness (1 John 1:9).

This is recognized as sound doctrine among all who call themselves fundamental believers. Yet many fail to recognize the fact that the same Bible says, I wish above all things that thou mayest prosper and be in health, even as thy soul prospereth (3 John 2). Health is God's will for His people, conditional on the well being of the soul.

God's promises are conditional

Salvation is conditional on repentance. Healing is conditional on faith and spiritual health. But when God's conditions are known and met, heaven guarantees the answer. For all the promises of God in him are yea, and in him Amen, unto the glory of God (2 Corinthians 1:20). For he is faithful that promised (Hebrews 10:23).

Many fail to receive healing because they do not ask for the definite thing they desire from God. Ye have not, because ye ask not (James 4:2).

The Bible tells of two blind men who were sitting by the wayside. When they heard that Jesus was passing by, they cried out, Have mercy on us, O Lord, thou Son of David. Truly, they were addressing their plea to the right Person, but when their prayer is analyzed, they really hadn't asked Him for anything specific! Jesus asked them, What will ye that I shall do unto you? They replied, Lord, that our eyes may be opened. Then their prayer was definite and immediately their eyes received sight (see Matthew 20:30–34).

When you come to God for healing, state your specific need. God's promise says, Whatsoever ye shall ask in my name, that will I do (John 14:13).

In one of my healing services, a man came who was deaf in one ear, blind in one eye, and had rheumatism in his knees. He asked for deliverance for his ear, which had been totally deaf for a number of years. As prayer was offered and Satan's power was broken, he immediately received his hearing. This so inspired his faith that he had courage to ask for healing of his eye. When this prayer was also answered, his faith was strengthened further, and he asked and received deliverance for his crippled knees. There was no new need in the man, or a new willingness on God's part to heal him. But as each need was specifically presented - definitely - God was true to His Word and did exactly what was asked in Jesus' name.

Often, the failure to make a specific request is because

of a lack of faith. A beggar at your door may say, "Please give me something to eat." He isn't sure that he will get anything. And if he should get something, he doesn't know what it will be. So he doesn't make a specific request. But when we go to the grocery store with money in our purse, we don't say, "Give me something to eat." We say, "Give me a loaf of bread and a pound of butter." We give the grocer a very definite list of just the things we want and the quantity of each. We have no doubt that we will receive the things we ask for.

Likewise, the person who comes to God believing that whatsoever he asks he shall receive, will usually ask for the specific things he desires.

Many times, if we can persuade the person seeking healing to determine in his mind exactly what he needs and expects to receive, and get him to ask for that specific healing, the barrier to healing is immediately removed.

If it be Thy will

Many people believe that it is a sign of meekness or humility to add to their prayer, "If it be thy will." However, this may be a trick of the enemy to keep you from having the faith to be healed. As long as you are not sure that it is God's will to heal you, you cannot ask in faith. Never, in the history of answered prayer, has anyone persuaded God to do anything contrary to his will! The secret of answered prayer is praying in His will.

Those who pray this way are following the example of the prayer of Jesus in Gethsemane, when He cried out in agony, If thou be willing, remove this cup from me: nevertheless not my will, but thine, be done (Luke 22:42). However, He was not praying for something that God had promised. He was not praying with a desire to change the circumstance. And, although the Son of God himself prayed this prayer, it did not bring about the change suggested in the prayer! This was never intended to be a prayer to change things. It was simply the agonizing cry of a struggling soul.

How different was the triumphant prayer at the tomb of Lazarus. *Father, I thank thee that thou hast heard me. And I knew that thou hearest me always...Lazarus, come forth!* (John 11:41–43).

When we pray for healing, we are praying for that which God has already revealed to be His will. Why, then, should we say, "If it be thy will"?

It is good to seek the will of God and pray in accordance with His will. James 4:13,15 says, *Go to now, ye that say, To day or to morrow we will go into such a city, and continue there a year, and buy and sell, and get gain: For that ye ought to say, If the Lord will, we shall live, and do this, or that.* In this case, God had not promised or revealed His will in the matter.

But God has promised and revealed His will in regard to the healing of His people. Therefore, we need not say, "If it be thy will." Rather, let us say, "I thank you, Father, that You have revealed Your will concerning this matter in Your Word, and I know I am asking in Your will."

And this is the confidence that we have in him, that, if we ask any thing according to his will, he heareth us: And if we know that he hear us, whatsoever we ask, we know that we have the petitions that we desired of him (1 John 5:14–15).

The "if" in many prayers not only denotes doubt, but it is used as a loophole to escape any possible charge of unbelief or unconfessed sin. If healing fails to come, the seeker can always use the excuse, "It just wasn't God's will to heal me. He heals others but, although I am blameless, God has shown respect of persons and chooses not to heal me."

In light of God's own plain statement that He is not a respecter of persons (see Romans 2:11), such a statement might well be considered slander against God, or "charging God foolishly."

Understand how God works

Many continue to suffer because they do not understand how God moves to bring about healing. They have their minds set about how God is going to do it. If the answer doesn't come according to their mental plan, they may lose confidence in God, or feel that their prayer was not heard and will not be answered. Since healing can only come by faith, it is important to understand how God works so that your faith won't be shaken.

Many people have remarked that, if God does the healing, it will be instantly complete. This is merely man's theory, for Jesus did not always heal this way. Although He did heal instantly and even today heals instantly and completely, it has not been a consistent pattern, for other patterns are also apparent in the ministry of Christ.

A certain nobleman, whose son was sick at Capernaum, met Jesus and said to Him, Come down ere my child die. Jesus said unto him: Go thy way; thy son liveth. According to the words of Jesus, the boy was healed - the work was done. The case was closed as far as Jesus was concerned. The nobleman's servants met him along the road before he reached home, bringing him the glad news, Thy son liveth. When the father inquired of them the hour when his boy began to mend, the servant replied, Yesterday at the seventh hour the fever left him. Then the father remembered that it was the same hour that Jesus had said, Thy son liveth (see John 4:49–51).

Note that the boy began to amend (verse 52). It would appear that, although this boy was truly healed, it was not an instant, full restoration to his former state of health and vigor. But rather, the fever left and he was on the road to recovery.

So it is today. In many cases, the cause of the disease is driven out, yet time is required before normal processes of growth or convalescence can bring about a state of full and normal well being. There are two dangers in failing to understand this truth.

First, you may lose confidence in the healing power of God, due to the disappointment of not being made perfectly whole as expected. This loss of confidence opens the door for Satan to return and again take possession of that which was taken from him (see Matthew 12:43–45). Then that which was gained is lost. This also accounts for those who testify of receiving a "partial healing," only to later be in a condition as bad or worse than they had before.

The second danger is that of accepting the partial deliverance as being all that God is going to do in your case. When this happens, you fail to continue standing against the devil, by faith, until the healing is complete. In this way, Satan hinders you from receiving all that God intended for you to have. God's plan is to bring complete healing, whether it be instant healing or a convalescent-type of deliverance.

If you do not receive instant healing, do not be discouraged. Keep praising God, by faith, for that which has already been done on your behalf - not just for the improvement in your condition, but for the stripes He bore at the whipping post in Jerusalem to pay the price for your deliverance! Keep right on looking to Jesus until the manifestation of your deliverance is complete.

As Jesus entered into a certain village, ten men who were lepers stood afar off and lifted up their voices, and said, Jesus, Master, have mercy on us. And when he saw them, he said unto them, Go shew yourselves unto the priest (Luke 17:13–14).

Jesus did not tell them they were healed right there on the spot. But He did tell them to go shew themselves to the priest, which they knew they had no right to do unless they were healed. In obedience and by faith, they started to the priest. They were doing the thing they could not do unless they were healed, even though there was not as yet any outward manifestation of their healing. It came to pass, that, as they went, they were cleansed (verse 14).

This was not an immediate, visible healing, but was a

genuine healing by the power of God. These men took God at His word, and His word did not fail. They acted on their faith, while the healing was not yet seen. And, as a result, they soon saw what they had faith to believe.

Act in faith

If you will do, by faith, that which you could not do before, God will meet you. Jesus frequently asked those who were bedfast to take up thy bed, and walk (John 5:8). And when they did, they were healed. At the beautiful gate of the temple, Peter said to the man who had been impotent in his feet from birth, In the name of Jesus Christ of Nazareth rise up and walk. And he took him by the right hand, and lifted him up: and immediately his feet and anklebones received strength. And he leaping up stood, and walked and entered with them into the temple, walking, and leaping (Acts 3:6–8). Many today are receiving deliverance in this exact same manner.

A young lady who had walked only on crutches for four years came seeking help in a healing line. As she came, the glow of faith was beaming upon her face. Before the minister could say one word to her, she handed him her crutches. She was fully persuaded, by faith, that she would need them no longer and, of course; she went away walking without them. God never fails to reward real living faith. Another came to the same healing line in a wheelchair. After prayer, she was commanded to rise and walk. Without making one effort to arise, she looked at the minister and said, "You know I can't do that." And she couldn't, because she did not believe. However, two nights later, after receiving more instruction on the promises of God, she did arise from the chair. She walked, ran, and climbed the steps to the platform. This type of healing was common in the healing ministry of Jesus, and it is still in effect today.

Obey God's commands

Faith in God is more than faith in His promises. It is also faith in His commands. They are not always a simple test of faith, as in the preceding cases, but may be a test of obedience, as well.

In John 9:1, Jesus met a man who was blind from birth. Jesus made clay and anointed the eyes of the blind man with the clay. Then He gave him a command, Go, wash in the pool of Siloam (verse 7). The blind man did exactly as he was told. He went his way therefore, and washed, and came seeing.

The blind man's eyes were opened! When? When the man obeyed the command of Jesus and did what He told him to do. Thus we learn that healing may be down the road of obedience. Jesus can heal you in the same way today. It is important to recognize that this is scriptural.

I know of many cases where God dealt with certain individuals concerning obedience, and they were miraculously healed as soon as they obeyed God's voice. It is doubtful that any who stubbornly refuse to do God's bidding can have faith to receive healing.

In James 5:16, God gives this command to those who seek healing: Confess your faults one to another, and pray one for another, that ye may be healed. There is a strong inference here that, if one is unwilling to confess his faults, these secret sins may destroy his faith and hinder him from being healed. It has been my experience, both as pastor and evangelist, that some who are prayed for do not receive healing until they have first confessed their faults. Many have wronged others and are unwilling to confess it. It is little wonder that, with such a rebellious spirit, they cannot have real faith for deliverance. But God promises that, if these faults are confessed, both the sin and the sickness shall be taken away.

One day, Jesus cursed a fig tree because it produced no fruit. Apparently there was no change in the appearance of the tree at the moment. But the next day when Jesus and

His disciples passed that way again, Peter said to Jesus in amazement, Master, behold, the fig tree which thou is withered away. In this short time it had dried up from the roots, and was withered away (see Mark 11:12–21).

Some healings are gradual

Many diseases are healed in the same way. The "root" of the disease is cursed in the name of Jesus. If it is a cancer, tumor, goiter, or some other growth, it must either pass from the body or disintegrate into the blood stream and be carried away. It is easy to understand that the person could be truly healed and yet continue to suffer some discomfort during this process. For a short time, the suffering may be even more acute than before, as this dead foreign tissue is being separated and carried away.

At this point, many fail to recognize what is happening, and they cast away their confidence. They give open testimony to the, fact that they are not healed, that they are even worse, and fear they will die. All this fear, loss of faith, and acceptance of Satan's suggestions, opens the door for Satan to replace in their bodies the very thing, which had been cast out by the power of God. So the healing is lost before any of its benefits are even recognized.

Although many cases of cancer are healed in this way, I have also known of many instances when cancer disappeared instantly after prayer.

God has no set pattern whereby He heals. Those who need healing must accept it God's way. God usually heals in the way that will bring the most glory to His name. Accept it just as He gives it. If it is instantaneous, shout the praises of God and go on your way rejoicing. If it is gradual, thank God for your healing just the same, and look joyfully to the time when you will be fully restored to health. If God has cursed the root of your disease, as He did with the fig tree, don't let your faith waver. Hold steady, knowing that it is your faith that maketh you whole.

But if God has commanded you to go, do, or speak, do not think that time alone will mend the matter. Be obedient to God and victory will come.

Perhaps you have had prayer for your healing once—or even many times—but failed to believe God for your healing. You think that perhaps it would denote unbelief to come back for prayer again for the same disease. Consider Mark 8:23–25. Here, Jesus took a blind man by the hand and led him out of the town. When He had spit on his eyes and put His hands upon him. He asked him if he saw aught. The man looked up and said, I see men as trees, walking. It was only after Jesus had laid His hands upon him the second time that his sight was fully restored. Then he saw every man clearly.

If you have had prayer and not received healing, do not be discouraged. Just start over. Start reading the New Testament as though it were a new book. Read and study this book, just as though you knew nothing at all about divine healing. You have missed an important point somewhere along the line, so just go back and start at the beginning. Be very careful to follow God's instructions in every detail and, as you do, heaven guarantees the answer.

Death is yet unconquered

The Bible teaches that we shall prosper and be in health even as our souls prosper. Yet we have no promise in the Word of God that divine healing will give unlimited physical life to any person in this present age. It is still true that it is appointed unto men once to die, but after this the judgment (Hebrews 9:27).

Some earnest teachers, preachers, and Christian people, in their great zeal to uphold the doctrine of healing, have left the strong inference that, if one should exercise sufficient faith, he might never die physically. But the Word of God makes it clear that death remains an unconquered enemy. The last enemy that shall be destroyed is death (1 Corinthians 15:26). A careful study of this scripture and its context will show that, while death will eventually be destroyed, destruction awaits a future time. The sting of death is sin. To the person who is saved from sin, death has lost its sting. But death itself is yet unconquered. Until Jesus returns and puts all things under Him, death remains the normal end of all mankind.

Some quote Romans 5:12–14 as proof that physical health can be ours indefinitely to the extent that there should be no physical death, but rather spiritual death - spiritual separation from God. One can be alive physically, but dead spiritually. But she that liveth in pleasure is dead while she liveth (1 Timothy 5:6). A careful study of Romans 5 (especially verses 17–19) will reveal that Paul was speaking of this spiritual death and not of physical death. For as by one man's disobedience many were made sinners, so by the obedience of one shall many be made righteous (verse 19). If the death spoken of in verses 12 and 14 is physical death, then verse 19 should read, "So by the obedience of one shall many be made immune from physical death."

It is true that physical health during our appointed lifetime has been provided in the atonement. But the Word does not teach that any person can have such outstanding faith as to never die physically. Only those whose normal life spans reach to the time when Jesus returns can escape a physical death. For those who are alive and remain shall be caught up...to meet the Lord in the air (1 Thessalonians 4:17).

The days of our years are threescore years and ten; and if by reason of strength they be fourscore years, yet is their strength labour and sorrow; for it is soon cut off, and we fly away (Psalm 90:10).

After giving this general rule regarding the normal length of life, God gives us this prayer pattern. So teach us to number our days, that we may apply our hearts unto wisdom (Psalm 90:12). According to this verse, even the most consecrated Christian should expect to come, at last, to the end of his days. This explains why some in advanced age fail to be raised from their beds. God's time may have come for them to go.

However, even if it should be the end of days for an individual, God's Word still does not indicate that it is His plan for that person to die in agony and disease. It is His desire that His servant should depart in peace (see Luke 2:29). Disease is not necessary to bring about death. God's pattern for death is found in Psalm 104:29: Thou takest away their breath, they die, and return to their dust.

Even when the time has come to die, there is scriptural basis for believing that, with unusual faith, a limited amount of time may be added to one's life. Hezekiah was informed that God had commanded him to set his house in order, for he should die and not live. Yet in answer to his leading, Hezekiah was granted an extension of life for fifteen years (see 2 Kings 20:1–5). Nevertheless, even though Hezekiah was healed and his life extended, when the fifteen years were over, he still had to die. Divine healing does not set aside the law of death. Real faith can only be based upon the Word of the One who is faithful. We can have faith for healing because God has promised healing. But God has not promised that this physical life shall continue indefinitely.

Accept your healing, God's way

Build your faith on the Word of God. Search the Word to find the reason you have not been healed. Get rid of the problem, and then accept your healing joyfully, in whatever way God sees fit to give it.

God may choose to heal you instantly, or He may choose to let the healing be gradual. He may choose to give a sudden manifestation of your healing, but at a little later time. Or, as in the case of one whose time has come to go, He may bring deliverance from pain and suffering by taking the person to his eternal rest.

Lay aside your own ideas of how God is going to heal you and accept the healing God's way. Believe God and take Him at His word. God says healing is for you. God, who cannot lie, says to believe that ye receive it and ye shall have it.

Do not cast away your confidence if recovery doesn't come immediately. Hold fast to your faith in the Word of God. Stand upon the promise and God guarantees that your healing shall come.

CHAPTER 10
HOW TO RECEIVE YOUR HEALING

On the Jericho road sat a blind man named Bartimaeus. He was a beggar. Bartimaeus had heard how Jesus had healed the sick, opened the blind eyes, and caused the dumb tongues to praise the Lord. But this was his first opportunity to meet Christ. When Bartimaeus learned that Jesus was passing by, he cried out, Jesus, thou son of David, have mercy on me (Mark 10:47). Bartimaeus had met with no opposition as, day by day; he sat by the road, cup in hand. People never meet with opposition as long as they suffer and are patient in their afflictions. But when one begins to cry out to Christ for help—pressing his way through to victory—all Satan's forces are turned upon him in opposition. However, greater is he that is in you, than he that is in the world (1 John 4:4). Jesus said, I give you power...over all the power of the enemy (Luke 10:19). Do not be defeated. Christ within you is greater than the power of the enemy that is in the world.

Do not give up. Be persistent.

The moment Bartimaeus cried out to the Lord for help, many charged him that he should hold his peace (Mark 10:48). They were trying their best to, discourage Bartimaeus from receiving his healing.

Notice the faith of Bartimaeus (verse 48). He would not be discouraged. He was determined to have his eye's opened. He knew that Jesus was the only one who could help. The more people tried to discourage him the louder he cried, Thou son of David, have mercy on me.

When Jesus saw that Bartimaeus would not be discouraged, He stopped and commanded him to be called. When they brought him to Jesus, He said to him, What wilt thou that I should do unto thee? Bartimaeus replied, Lord, that I might receive my sight.

Then Jesus said unto him, Go thy way; thy faith hath made thee whole. And immediately he received his sight, and followed Jesus in the way (Mark 10:52).

Had Bartimaeus listened to the people, he would have been turned away and never been healed.

God is the rewarder of them that diligently seek Him (Hebrews 11:6). One must not be discouraged. A real determination to persist until victory comes is very important. If a person has prayed through to real victory before he enters the prayer line, nothing will discourage him. He will press right on until he receives healing.

Remember Calvary

David said, Bless the LORD, O my soul and forget not all his benefits (Psalm 103:2). That means, "remember all His benefits." To be reminded of all God's benefits, we must go back to Calvary. The benefits mentioned by David include forgiveness of all sins and healing of all diseases—not part of our sins or part of our diseases, but ALL—every sin and every disease! This is the benefit of Calvary.

Seven hundred years before Calvary, Isaiah looked forward to the cross. Upon that cross he saw a man dying —shedding His blood—for the sins of the world. But He was dying with His back bruised and bleeding from the stripes, which He bore that we might be set free from sickness as well as sin. Speaking as he was moved by the Holy Ghost, Isaiah cried out in Prophetic utterance, He is despised and rejected of men; a man of sorrows, and acquainted with grief: and we hid as it were our faces from him; he was despised, and we esteemed him not. Surely he hath borne our griefs, and carried our sorrows: yet we did esteem him stricken, smitten of God, and afflicted. But he was wounded for our transgressions, he was bruised for our iniquities: the chastisement of our peace was upon him; and with his stripes we are healed (Isaiah 53:3–5). So, at Calvary, we are healed by His stripes.

Sixty years after Calvary, the Apostle Peter declared, Who his own self bare our sins in his own body on the tree, that we, being dead to sins, should live unto righteousness: by whose stripes ye were healed (1 Peter 2:24).

What difference does it make whether it is sixty years after Calvary or nineteen hundred years after Calvary? Time cannot change God's eternal Word. The fact remains that, at Calvary, ye were healed! The work was finished there. All God asks us to do is to believe it, then receive it.

Only as a sinner believes in Calvary for the atonement of his soul can he receive salvation from sin. And only as you, dear sick and suffering friend, believe in the stripes can you receive healing for your body. Jesus Christ shed His blood to atone for all sins. The sufferings of His body were not for that purpose.

Forasmuch as ye know that ye were not redeemed with corruptible things, as silver and gold, from your vain conversation received by tradition from your fathers; But with the precious blood of Christ, as of a lamb without blemish and without spot (1 Peter 1:18–19).

In whom we have redemption through his blood, the forgiveness of sins, according to the riches of his grace (Ephesians 1:7).

For the life of the flesh is in the blood: and I have given it to you upon the altar to make an atonement for your souls: for it is the blood [not the flesh] that maketh an atonement for the soul (Leviticus 17:11).

Christ did not suffer in His body for our sins. He shed His blood for that. The stripes were for our healing! David says so. Isaiah says so. Peter says so. Christ himself says that it is so and that should be sufficient.

Thanks be to God for Calvary! At Calvary, we find atonement for the soul. But we cannot stop there, for that is merely half of the benefits of Calvary. The other half is healing for the physical body.

Many today have forgotten His benefits. Many remember part of His benefits, but they have forgotten the part that provides deliverance for our physical bodies. As far as they are concerned, they make the sufferings of Christ to be in vain. Paul refers to this very thing when he tells us why Christians are sick. For this cause many are weak and sickly among you, and many sleep [die prematurely] (1 Corinthians 11:30). The cause is found in verse 29 - failure to discern the Lord's body. That is, not understanding, or failing to remember that His body was bruised and broken so we could be healed. In this scripture, Paul is referring to the sacrament. Going back to the teaching of Christ on this same subject, we find that Jesus took bread and blessed it and brake it and gave it to the disciples. He said, Take, eat, this is my body (Matthew 26:26). In verses 27 and 28, He took the cup, and gave thanks and gave it unto them saying, Drink ye all of it; For this is my blood of the new testament, which is shed for many for the remission of sins. Here Christ shows a distinction between the body and the blood. This distinction is the reason that both the bread and the wine are included in the symbolism of the sacrament. The wine symbolizing the blood shed for our sins and the bread symbolizing the body broken for the healing of our sicknesses. Failing to discern the Lord's body (see 1 Corinthians 11:29) means forgetting half of Calvary's benefits - failing to remember that it was by His stripes that ye are healed (see Isaiah 53:5). No wonder so many were weak and sickly in the church at Corinth. They neglected the provision God had made for their healing. And it is for this same reason that many Christian people are weak and sick today. They have forgotten the benefits of Calvary.

Jesus' last words on the cross, before He gave up the ghost, were, It is finished (John 19:30). What did He mean? He meant just this: He had borne the sins of the world and carried its sorrows. Himself took our infirmities, and bare our sicknesses (Matthew 8:17).

Since Christ bore your sicknesses, you no longer have to be sick. You can be released from sin and sickness by remembering that Christ finished your redemption from both—once and for all—at Calvary.

It's time to be healed!

Now you are ready to come for prayer, believing that the moment hands are laid upon you in Jesus' name, according to His word, you, shall recover. For Jesus said, These signs shall follow them that believe...they shall lay hands on the sick, and they shall recover (Mark 16:17–18). Also remember that James said, The prayer of faith shall save the sick, and the Lord shall raise him up.

The moment hands are laid upon you, remember Calvary and claim every one of its benefits. Begin, by faith, to act healed. Start doing the things your affliction kept you from doing.

It is important to recognize that the one who is laying hands upon the sick is doing so under divine authority. Remember that this believer has been authorized by Christ to loose you from your infirmities. Christ has given him power and authority over your affliction. He is acting under divine commission. Christ himself said, Behold, I give unto you power...over all the power of the enemy (Luke 10:19). He...gave them power and authority over all devils, and to cure diseases (Luke 9:1).

The man of God who is to bring deliverance to you has full faith in Calvary's victory over Satan. He believes in the power of the blood to cleanse from sin. And he believes in the power of the broken body of Christ to set you free from sickness. He believes it because God, who cannot lie, said, These signs shall follow them that believe; In my name shall they cast out devils; they shall speak with new tongues...they shall lay hands on the sick, and they shall recover! (Mark 16:17–18). He knows that, in the name of Jesus, Satan must retreat. By faith, he can bind, rebuke, and command Satan to remove the affliction, in the name of Jesus, and Satan must respect that name! And the victory at Calvary applies to your case. So what is the next step?

Believe

Just simply believe! Believing is faith. Faith does not just know that God is able. Faith is believing that God does it. You believe it simply because God said He would do it, and you know that God cannot lie.

Faith is the substance of things hoped for, the evidence of things not seen (Hebrews 11:1). Faith is reaching out into the unseen, getting hold of that which is not, and holding on until it becomes that which is. Faith is believing that we possess that which we cannot see or feel. Although it is as yet unseen and unfelt, we believe it is already done. This kind of faith brings deliverance!

Believe, even though you are in pain. Believe, even though you have tried to walk and could not! Keep on believing and trying to act upon your faith. It is believing that drives out the pain and brings you forth from your bed.

The unbeliever says, "Let me feel and I will believe."

God says, "Believe, and I will let you feel."

Real faith is believing without being able to feel. We are healed according to our faith, not according to our feeling. Feeling comes after faith has been exercised. So do not look for feeling, look for healing!

Faith for healing is believing absolutely that we are healing in spite of such things as weakness or pain. It is simply believing that we already have the thing for which we prayed before we see it or feel it. This is exactly what John meant when he said, This is the confidence that we have in him, that, if we ask anything according to his will, he heareth us: And if we know that he hear us, whatsoever we ask, we know that we have the petitions that we desired of him (1 John 5:14–15).

Faith without works is dead (James 2:20). In other words, faith that doesn't work is dead. Since real faith is alive, it is active faith. It works—it acts. When you absolutely believe that by His stripes you were heard, you begin to act on God's word. Joy comes into your heart as the realization of what God has done for you sweeps over your soul. Faith always brings rejoicing. As you rejoice in your victory, stand upon your feet! Rise up, in Jesus' name, and walk! Do the thing that you could not do. Leave your wheelchair. Throw away your crutches. Walk and run and leap for joy! Speak! Hear! See out of obscurity and darkness. Do it in Jesus' name. Because you believe, you are healed and you can and will do the things you could not do.

Act your faith

Step out on the promise of God. Quit talking about your faith and begin to act your faith. If you have real faith, you won't have to tell people about it—they can see it.

Four men brought a palsied friend to Jesus to be healed. They had faith that could be seen. And when he saw their faith, he said unto him, Man, thy sins are forgiven thee (Luke 5:20).

People who have real faith act, instead of bragging and talking. Do not declare that you have "all the faith in the world," when you are still sick and afflicted. If you have that much faith, you ought to be bringing deliverance to the multitudes of sick and suffering people!

Do not say, "If I can only believe." Leave the "if" out. Quit "trying to believe." Simply believe and act on the Word of God. Be ye DOERS of the word, and not hearers only, deceiving your own selves (James 1:22).

Talk about your healing. Talk about the goodness of God. Talk about God's promises. Quote every scripture promise of healing you know.

Do not talk about your failure and defeat. Quit talking about your doubts. Quit talking about your pains. Throw away your medicines. Quit telling people what a wonderful job the devil has done of blinding you with sickness. Quit glorifying the devil and testifying to his power.

Speak of your faith in God's promises. Tell people what a wonderful work the Lord Jesus has done in making you whole and driving away the power of Satan. Let your testimony glorify God. We overcome the devil by the word of our testimony (see Revelation 12:11).

At this point, someone might say, "But Brother Allen, I have pain." The pain declares that the sickness is not healed. But we care not what your pain declares or what your feelings say. God's Word says by his stripes ye were healed! God's Word declares one thing. Your pain declares another. Which are you going to believe—God's Word or your pain? What do you declare? What is your testimony? This is what it should be: "BY HIS STRIPES I AM HEALED!"

Some might think this is a lie, but it is not, for God's Word cannot lie.

Many times, after a person has gone through a healing line, a friend or loved one who is standing close by will ask, "How do you feel? Do you really feel any better? Can you hear out of that ear now?" They are unaware of the fact that they are helping the devil.

Don't let the devil make you think or talk in terms of what you feel, unless your feelings agree with what God says. Feelings are good if they agree with the Word of God. But God's Word is greater than your feelings. If your feelings do not yet agree with the Word of God, ignore them. Refuse to speak of them. Quote God's Word instead. Stand on it by faith and tell those who ask, "By His stripes I am healed."

You do not have to lie about your pains. It is wrong to lie. Do not say, "The pain is gone," when the pain is still there. Do not say, "I can hear everything clearly," when you cannot. If you feel bad, it is a lie to say, "I feel good." If you still have pain, don't lie about it - just refuse to discuss it. Quote God's Word, for it is truth. Real faith must be based exclusively upon the Word of God. You are not to believe that you are healed because the pain is gone. And you shouldn't refuse to believe that you are healed because you still feel the pain. That pain has nothing to do with your faith. Feeling is not faith and faith is not feeling. Faith is believing that you are healed because God says that you are healed!

If a person should say, "I believe I got healed because the pain is gone," that person would immediately lose faith should any sign of that pain return. Then he would say, I thought that I was healed, but I was not. The pain is back again."

Faith is never afraid to take a stand with the Word of God. Let God be true and every man a liar (Romans 3:4). If our feelings do not agree with what God say, then our feelings lie. A person who walks by faith ignores the testimony of his senses, unless it agrees with the Word of God.

Make this your testimony: "God says it is done. I believe it...it is done! It is finished. I am healed because God, who cannot lie, declares that I am healed!"

This is the way to receive healing. It comes, not by feeling, but by faith. If you follow these steps, God guarantees to heal you!

CHAPTER 11
WHO HAS POWER TO HEAL?

During His earthly ministry, Jesus healed all manner of sickness and all manner of disease among the people (Matthew 4:23).

The glorious ministry of deliverance that Jesus began was to continue through His disciples, followers, and believers.

Jesus called His twelve disciples and gave them power against unclean spirits, to cast them of sickness and all out, and to heal all manner of disease (Matthew 10:1). Then He sent them forth to preach the kingdom of God, and to heal the sick (Luke 9:2).

After these things the Lord appointed other seventy also, and sent them...into every city and place (Luke 10:1) He commanded these seventy to preach the gospel, but that was not all He commanded them to do. He also told them to heal the sick that are therein, and say unto them, "The kingdom of God is come nigh unto you" (verse 9).

At the close of this journey, the seventy returned to Jesus with joy, saying, "Even the devils are subject unto us through thy name" (verse 17).

Before Jesus went back to heaven, He left with His followers this mighty promise: "Verily, verily I say unto you, He that believeth on me, the works that I do shall he do also; and greater works than these shall he do; because I go unto my Father" (John 14:12).

Many preachers who deny the miracle-working power of Jesus Christ in His church today admit that Christ healed the sick, but declare that the day of miracles is past. They say that the sick cannot be healed by the power of God today because Jesus is gone. But He plainly stated that His going did not mean the end of miracles, but rather that miracles would increase.

Fulfilling The Great Commission

His last commission to those He left behind to carry on His work was, "Go ye into all the world, and preach the gospel to every creature. He that believeth and is baptized shall be saved; but he that believeth not shall be damned. And these signs shall follow them that believe; In my name shall they cast out devils, they shall lay hands on the sick, and they shall recover" (Mark 16:15–18). Matthew adds, "Teaching them to observe all things whatsoever I have commanded you: and, lo, I am with you alway, even unto the end of the world" (Matthew 28:20).

According to Mark, as soon as He had spoken these words, Jesus was received up into heaven, and sat on the right hand of God. "And they [the disciples to whom He gave this commission] went forth, and preached everywhere, the Lord working with them, and confirming the word with signs following" (Mark 16:19–20). This was the fulfillment of His promise in Matthew 28:20.

Although it is true that He is in heaven, it is certainly scriptural to say that He is still with those who believe and preach His gospel, for He said He would be, even unto the end of the world! He is with them, confirming His word with the same signs following that are listed in Mark 16:17–18.

After Christ ascended into heaven, the Church was born on the day of Pentecost (see Acts 2). That Church, filled with the power of the Holy Ghost and endued with the gifts of the Spirit, continued the same ministry that Christ had begun. The Spirit-filled followers of Jesus continued His glorious ministry of deliverance even after He had returned to heaven.

A certain man lame from his mother's womb was carried, whom they laid daily at the gate of the temple which is called Beautiful (Acts 3:2). When Peter and John came by, they said, "Look on us." Peter continued, "Silver and gold have I none; but such as I have give I thee: In the name of Jesus Christ of Nazareth rise up and walk" (Acts 3:6). "Peter took him by the hand and lifted him up and immediately his feet and anklebones received strength. And he leaping up stood, and walked, and entered with them into the temple, walking, and leaping, and praising God" (verse 8).

The people were filled with wonder and amazement at this mighty miracle, which they had witnessed. They had thought (even as do many church members today) that, since Christ himself was gone from earth, they would see no more miracles. Many of them began to ascribe divinity to those through whose hands the miracle had been wrought. Peter, with rare but commendable humility, stopped them immediately, saying, "Ye men of Israel, why marvel ye at this?" Or why look ye so earnestly on us, as though by our own power or holiness we had made this man to walk. His [Jesus] name through faith in his name hath made this man strong, whom ye see and know: yea, the faith which is by him hath given him this perfect soundness in the presence of you all" (verses 12,16).

No man has this power in himself. But it is available to every believer. All of the power which Christ used is available to His followers today. The things He did while in His earthly body are a pattern for those He left in the world to complete the work He began (see 1 Peter 2:21–24). The gifts of the Spirit, listed in 1 Corinthians 12, and the commandments of Christ to His followers, cover all the miracles that Christ ever performed. He used no power, which He did not make available to His followers - even unto the end of the world.

Stephen was a deacon in the first church. But he was "full of faith, and power [and], did great wonders and miracles among the people" (Acts 6:8).

Philip, another of the first deacons, went down to Samaria and preached Christ there. "And the people with one accord gave heed unto those things which Philip spake, hearing and seeing the miracles which he did. For unclean spirits, crying with loud voice, came out of many that were possessed with them: and many taken with palsies, and that were lame, were healed" (Acts 8:6–7).

Twenty-nine years after the ascension of Christ, Paul was still healing the sick (see Acts 28:8–9). Although Paul was not among those who heard the commission and promises of Jesus on the Mount of Olives before He ascended, "God wrought special miracles by the hands of Paul: So that from his body were brought unto the sick handkerchiefs or aprons, and the diseases departed from them, and the evil spirits went out of them" (Acts 19:11–12).

Miracles By Handkerchiefs And Aprons

Countless thousands are being healed today by the ministry of blessed (anointed) cloths. God has made this provision for the sake of those who cannot get out to seek help. Although we cannot reach them and lay hands upon them personally, we can send them a cloth that our hands have touched. This is God's scriptural method for ministering to those who are sick, bound, and afflicted. When they cannot get into direct contact with those whose faith is strong, and whom the Lord is using in this ministry, they can make contact through a cloth. Just as the ministry of blessed cloths brought deliverance to thousands in Paul's day, it is still bringing miraculous deliverance today. Thousands of miracles are taking place today through this simple ministry. God's method of deliverance for those who are sick is still the same today. This method of sending forth cloths from the bodies of God's anointed ministers is still effective.

God has no respect of persons. Those who are sick should receive these cloths in faith and follow the same instructions as those who stand in healing lines. When this cloth is laid upon the body of the afflicted person, he would exercise the same faith as if he were in a healing line, with hands actually being laid upon his body. If he will do this, the same results will follow in every case.

These cloths, received in faith, bear the same virtue and power that the hands of the evangelist bear. This is scriptural provision that God has made for the countless thousands who cannot attend the divine healing services that are being conducted across the country today.

If the blessed cloth is for yourself, do not place it upon your body until you have carefully followed the instructions in this book. Then, and only then, place it upon your body in faith, believing God for a miraculous deliverance the moment it touches your body. If you are sending the cloth to a loved one or friend who is afflicted, you should take responsibility to give proper instruction in the way of faith yourself, or send instructions like this book, so that he may acquire the necessary faith for deliverance.

Before you request a prayer cloth for someone else, be sure that he has the faith that God gives. The same faith is required, whether it be the cloth that is laid upon him or the hands of the evangelist. Remember that it is faith on the part of the sick person that brings deliverance, as well as the faith of the one who has laid hands upon the cloth. Only by faith can anything be received from God. Where there is faith in God's faithfulness, God guarantees to heal you!

The miracles of Paul became so outstanding that even some whose lives had not been purified by faith came to believe that miracles could surely be done in the name of Jesus (see Acts 19:13–18). These people had not made contact with Jesus themselves, but knew Him only as "Jesus, whom Paul preacheth." When they attempted to cast out demons in that name, they were recognized by the demons as having no authority. They believed what they had seen - the miracles that they had seen Paul perform. But they did not have faith in God. They did not believe that God would work miracles by their hands because of His direct word to them. They did not prove their faith in God by believing His commands as well as His promises and by living lives of consecration and holiness.

Many sincere people today have met with disappointment and discouragement because they have tried to appropriate God's promises without taking care to fulfill His commands. The name of Jesus is not a charm - it possesses no magic. But it does possess power when used by those to whom He has given "power of attorney"—the right to do business for Him in His name. This power is for all who truly believe and act upon all of God's Word.

The Early Church was a powerful church because its members believed God. They believed in holy living because God said, "Be ye holy." They feared sin because they had seen sin revealed through the gift of discernment and liars struck dead for their sin (see Acts 5). They believed that they could do miracles in the name of Jesus because He had said, "The works that I do shall ye do also." And because they believed God, God worked with them, confirming His word with signs and wonders. God has not changed. Any church today can have the same power if they will meet the same conditions.

The Church At Work Today

Twenty-six years after the ascension of Christ, the Apostle Paul wrote to the church at Corinth, saying, "For God hath set some in the Church, first apostles, secondarily prophets, thirdly teachers, after that miracles, then gifts of healings" (1 Corinthians 12:28). That same Church is still at work in the world today and will be until the trumpet sounds and the first resurrection takes place and 1 Thessalonians 4:13–18 is fulfilled. Then the work of the Church on this earth will be complete, and it will rise to meet the Lord in the air. As long as that Church believes the Word of God, it shall continue to heal the sick and perform miracles in the mighty name of Jesus. Jesus declared, "These signs shall follow them that believe: they shall lay hands on the sick, and they shall recover" (Mark 16:16–17). The gifts of the Spirit—the performing of miracles and healing of the sick—has not been confined to just a few chosen people in the Early Church, or to a few preachers today. As long as there is a believer on the earth, miracles can be performed in the name of Jesus.

Nowhere in the Scriptures is the ministry of healing limited to any particular time, or to outstanding individuals. Even in the Old Testament, it was God's plan that all those whom He had set as shepherds over His people should heal the sick. "Woe be to the shepherds of Israel. The diseased have ye not strengthened, neither have ye healed that which was sick, neither have ye bound up that which was broken" (Ezekiel 34:2,4).

There was more power in Elisha's dead bones (see 2 Kings 13:21) than there is in some preachers who are very much alive today. Although only one man was healed by coming in contact with Elisha's bones, still that is more than can be said for the entire lifetime of many who call themselves the shepherds of God's flock today.

If God was displeased with the shepherds of Israel who did not heal the sick, what must His attitude be toward the shepherds of His New Testament church who, having His commission to do the works that He did, not only refuse to heal the sick, but criticize and persecute those who do!

There was more power in Peter's shadow than in the bodies of many of those who claim to be his successors in ministering to the church of Jesus Christ (see Acts 5).

There was more power in handkerchiefs and aprons which had come in contact with the body of Paul than in many great "fundamental" religious bodies today (see Acts 19:11–12).

Has God changed? No! The Church that Jesus purchased with His blood is still performing miracles and healing the sick. Those who dare to believe God's promises and stand on His word can still heal the sick in the name of Jesus. God has given those who believe "authority over all devils, and to cure diseases" (Luke 9:1).

Many will declare that only God has authority over devils and to cure diseases. In one sense this is true. But it is also true that God chose to delegate that authority to His Son. Accepting that authority from the Father, Jesus, during His earthly ministry, commanded demons, unclean spirits, and diseases to depart. They recognized His authority and were obedient to Him. Just before He returned to heaven, Jesus delegated that same authority to those who believe in His name. This gives the true believer the right to use the name of Jesus in making requests of God and in giving commands to demons and diseases (see John 14:10–14). Thus the works that Jesus did while He was here on earth can be continued in His absence. When the believer accepts this authority and uses the name of Jesus reverently, the effect is the same as if Jesus himself had spoken, for God will honor such prayers and commands. The believer has no power of his own and can do nothing in his own name, but all things are subject to the name of Jesus.

Those who attempt to use His name without being qualified by believing and being obedient to Jesus will see no results and may be penalized for "forgery," as were the seven sons of Sceva (see Acts 19:14–16).

Word Of Command

There are very few scriptures that refer to praying for the sick. In most cases, a few words of command, spoken by the one having authority, was all that was needed. Jesus did not pray for the sick. He healed the sick, and commanded the demons to depart. Peter and John did not pray for the man at the beautiful gate of the temple. They commanded him, in the name of Jesus Christ of Nazareth, to rise up and walk (see Acts 3:6). Paul first prayed, then laid his hands upon Publius' father and healed him (see Acts 28:8). Demons and diseases are still subject to believers who command them in Jesus' name. Since I recognized this truth in God's Word, I have seen multitudes delivered from demons and set free from all manner of diseases at my command. These cases include cancers, goiters, tumors, sinus trouble, tuberculosis, asthma, heart disease, and many others. I do not claim that this is evidence of a special gift, or of special favor with God. It is simply done in Jesus' name and by the authority, which God has promised to them that believe.

Although, in the majority of cases, the word of command in Jesus' name is all that is necessary to bring deliverance, there are also scriptures that prove the necessity of prayer in some cases. If you have gone through a healing line where hands have been laid on you and your disease commanded to depart and you still do not receive deliverance, do not hesitate to take advantage of the provision in James 5:14–16. Your failure to be delivered may be the result of unconfessed sin. If this is the case, confess your faults and ask trusted elders to pray for you that you may be delivered from both sickness and sin.

When Miriam was stricken with leprosy as a result of her sin against Moses, she and her brother Aaron begged Moses to pray for her. He cried unto God, "Heal her now, O God, I beseech thee" (Numbers 12:13).

The true believer in the Lord Jesus Christ is aware that God will not heal an unrepentant sinner, or an enemy of the Cross. He will not knowingly use his authority to do anything which Jesus himself would not do if He were present in the body. Those who are still in bondage to sin should first seek help in prayer that they might be set free from sin. When they have done this, God's promise is definite. "The prayer of faith shall save the sick, and the Lord shall raise him up; and if he have committed sins, they shall be forgiven him" (James 5:15).

Casting Out Demons

Much sickness is a direct result of demon oppression (see Acts 10:38). Jesus did not say, "Pray for the demon oppressed and demon possessed." He said, "Cast out demons." Prayer alone will not drive out demons. Fasting and prayer, seeking the face of God, and repenting of all known sin is, in some cases, necessary to prepare the hearts of both the one seeking deliverance and the one coming in the name of the Lord to bring deliverance. In this way, they are made ready to enter the battle with Satan and claim victory over him. Until demons hear the word of command, given by faith in Jesus' name by one who has the authority to use that name, they will not move. They do not have to go and they know it.

Jesus' disciples once attempted to cast a demon out of a boy while Jesus was on the mountain fasting and praying.

They knew the power of Jesus' name. They had cast out demons before. They were sure this one would go. But this stubborn demon refused to go. They were much distressed by the apparent failure of the authority, which they understood to be theirs. But they were not content to say, "The time when we could work miracles is past." When Jesus had cast out the demon, they inquired of Him why they had failed. Jesus replied, "Because of your unbelief: for verily I say unto you, If ye have faith as a grain of mustard seed...nothing shall be impossible unto you. Howbeit this kind goeth not out but by prayer and fasting" (Matthew 17:20–21). These men had been given authority over demons, as long as they had faith. When faith was allowed to become dormant because of a lack of communion with God, they became powerless. Faith must be fed by frequent time alone with God, when all the demands of the flesh are set aside. Times of fasting and prayer keep our faith strong so we can overcome the power of Satan and bring deliverance to those who are oppressed or possessed of the devil.

Satan was defeated at Calvary, but he refuses to acknowledge defeat. He yields only when and what he must. The ground must be taken step by step. To be able to do this, the Spirit-filled minister today must have explicit faith in Calvary's victory over Satan. He must live his life avoiding sin and must not be concerned with any personal gain. He must stand only for God's right against Satan. There must be no uncrucified flesh in his life. Then, and only then, will Satan admit his defeat.

The Baptism Of The Holy Ghost

It is surprising, but some people today desire to exercise this power, yet they reject the source of that power - the baptism of the Holy Ghost. Jesus himself did no miracles and cast out no demons until, first, God anointed Him with the Holy Ghost and with power (see Acts 10:38; John 2:11).

His promise to the disciples was, "But ye shall receive power, after that the Holy Ghost is come upon you." (Acts 1:8).

If Jesus himself would not attempt this work alone and encouraged His disciples to wait until the Spirit had come to endue them with power from on high before attempting this work, surely those who would claim power and authority over demons and diseases today should first be filled with the Spirit.

The Early Church was a powerful church because it was a Spirit-filled, God-centered, God-fearing church. The phenomenal growth of that church from 120 (Acts 1:15) to 3,000 (Acts 2:41) to 5,000 (Acts 4:4) to "multitudes" (Acts 5:14) can only be attributed to one thing - the supernatural power of God was working. The gifts of the Spirit were in operation. The church loved God, feared sin, and was full of the Holy Ghost.

Only when God can find a group of people who answer this description today will revival come to this sin-blinded, human-controlled, self-sufficient, Christ-rejecting, pleasure-mad, movie-minded, cigarette-smoking, beer-guzzling, drink-and-dope-crazed, judgment-bound world.

Only when the Church again lifts its voice in one accord in repentance will God send a revival to sweep our land, as in days gone by. We must cry out like the Early Church, "And now, Lord, behold their threatenings: and grant unto thy servants, that with all boldness they may speak thy word, by stretching forth thine hand to heal; and that signs and wonders may be done by the name of thy holy child Jesus" (Acts 4:29–30). Then multitudes will again be saved, filled with the Holy Ghost, and healed by the power of God.

God has not withdrawn the delegation of His authority over demons and disease from those who believe His commands and promises and act upon their faith.

CHAPTER 12
KEEPING YOUR HEALING

God has not only guaranteed to heal you, He has also guaranteed to keep you healed. But, like the rest of God's promises, this promise is conditional. God tells us in His Word how to be healed and how to stay healed. Some, who did not realize that there was more to do after they received healing, soon found that they were no better off than if they had never been healed.

First, let us remember that, while not all sickness can be attributed to demon possession or even demon oppression, God is not the author of sickness. Satan is responsible, in one way or another, for all sickness. Satan is an active, crafty, intelligent enemy. He gives up no ground except that which is actively taken from him by faith. And having given up ground, he is constantly on the watch for an opportunity to take it back again. Jesus gave not only promises and commands, but warnings as well. One warning is found in Matthew 12:43–45: When the unclean spirit is gone out of a man, he walketh through dry places, seeking rest, and findeth none. Then he saith, I will return into my house from whence I came out; and when he is come, he findeth it empty, swept, and garnished. Then goeth he, and taketh with himself seven other spirits more wicked than himself, and they enter in and dwell there: and the last state of that man is worse than the first.

Give no place to the devil

When you have been released from the power of Satan, whether it is from sin, sickness, demon oppression, or demon possession, it is important that the house—which is your body, be not only clean, but also occupied. When Satan moves out, the Spirit of God must move in. Never let the devil find your house empty. If you have not yet been filled with the Holy Ghost, seek to be filled immediately and then stay filled. Let the Spirit of God dwell in you richly, keeping, directing, possessing, and using you for the glory of God. Then Satan cannot return.

Neither give place to the devil (Ephesians 4:27). The devil cannot move in unless we give him a place. Those who abide in Christ are safe from Satan's power. Be so filled with righteousness that there is no room for sin...so filled with faith that there is no room for doubt...so filled with the Spirit of God that there is no room for any other spirit to dwell there.

Sin and careless living on the part of one who has been healed is an open invitation for the unclean spirit to move back into the house from which he was driven. Jesus warned one whom He had healed, instantly and miraculously, with these words: Behold, thou art made whole: sin no more, lest a worse thing come unto thee (John 5:14).

The danger is not simply a matter of being no better, but of being even worse, for when the original demon returns, he may bring others with him. It is easy to see the importance of abiding in faith, feeding upon God's Word, keeping in communion with God through prayer, and resisting the devil.

Resist the devil, and he will flee from you (James 4:7).

The Christian need not be in subjection to sin. Sin shall not have dominion over you (Romans 6:14). By faith, the Christian has power to refuse the temptations of Satan and his suggestions to sin. There is something more commendable than daily repentance from sin and that is daily victory over sin.

It is also possible, by faith, to refuse to give sickness a place. There is something better than being healed "many times," especially of the same affliction, and that is to get healed and stay healed.

If you ever receive healing for your body it will be by faith. You will also stay healed by faith. Faith is joyful, and the sick person who lacks faith is sorrowful because of his pain and sickness. The sick person who has faith is joyful because he realizes that victory has already been bought, paid for, promised, and is on the way. He will rejoice and praise God from his heart, regardless of what he sees or feels.

This kind of faith cannot fail to bring healing. Satan knows that faith is his enemy and constantly strives to destroy it. Whenever you feel any pain, which remotely resembles the pain of your previous disease, Satan will immediately suggest to your mind that you were never healed, were not completely healed, or that your healing didn't last.

If you haven't heard from God for some time, and His promises are dim in your mind, you may find it easier to believe Satan than to believe God. If you do, you may even agree with Satan and say in your heart, "I just thought I was healed. I am no better." Your heart will be heavy and your faith will be shattered. Fear will come into your heart, and the door will be open for Satan to afflict you again.

But if the promises of God are bright and clear in your mind and you still believe that He meant just what He said, you will answer Satan, as did our Lord when He was tempted, It is written (Matthew 4:4,7,10). By whose stripes ye were healed (1 Peter 2:24). As you review the mighty promises of God, your heart will rejoice, even as it did when you claimed His promise and received healing. There will be praise in your heart to God for His mighty deliverance. Stand upon a promise in God's Word and praise God in the devil's face. This is resisting the devil. He never has and never will be able to stay in the presence of this kind of faith.

Stay in an atmosphere of faith

After you are healed, it is a mistake to go back into a church where the pastor and teachers do not believe in the miracle-working power of God. God describes these people and gives a warning concerning them in 2 Timothy 3:5, Having a form of godliness, but denying the power thereof; from such turn away. There are many good churches, where the full gospel is preached and the power of God is recognized and works for the healing of sick bodies as well as sin-sick souls. Identify yourself with one of these groups. There you will find food for your faith, and you can freely give your testimony for the encouragement of others who may also need deliverance.

Your testimony is important

As Christ entered a certain village, there met Him ten men who were lepers. They lifted up their voices and said, Jesus, Master, have mercy on us. When Christ saw them he said, Go shew yourselves to the priests. And it came to pass, that, as they went, they were cleansed (Luke 17:13–14). However, only one of the ten ever returned to give God thanks and glory for His deliverance. And one of them, when he saw that he was healed, turned back, and with a loud voice glorified God, and fell down on his face at his feet, giving him thanks. Christ asked the one who returned, Were there not ten cleansed? But where are the nine? (Verses 15–17).

There should have been ten returning to give God glory, in-as-much as there were ten who were miraculously healed. Only one out of ten came to give glory to Jesus for His healing. What were the other nine doing? The scripture does not tell us. But this lesson does teach us what the other nine should have done! They should have returned and glorified Christ!

Many people will attend services night after night until they can go through a healing line and receive healing for their body. But then they never return to testify of the miracle so that Christ may be glorified. There may be times when it is impossible for some to return and give their testimony. If this is the case, they should write their testimony and return it to those under whose ministry they were healed. How ungrateful and unthankful many people are today. This is evidenced when they fail to give their testimony.

When Jesus healed the man at Gadara, He said to him, Go home to thy friends, and tell them how great things the Lord hath done for thee, and hath had compassion on thee (Mark 5:19).

If you have been healed by the power of God, be sure to testify in every public meeting possible. Explain your past sickness and tell how long you suffered with it. If you received medical aid, explain the doctor's diagnosis and give all information possible to prove your healing, such as doctors' statements, photographs, x-rays, etc. Tell whether you were healed instantly or received a gradual healing.

Your testimony is important. Not only will it bless and encourage others to trust God for their deliverance, but also it will help you to overcome the devil. We overcome him [the devil] by the blood of the Lamb, and by the word of our testimony (Revelation 12:11). As you give testimony with your lips to the truth and reality of God's promises, your faith will increase, Satan will be driven farther back, and his chance of overcoming you again will decrease.

Resist the devil, keep full of God's Spirit, feed on God's Word, believe God's promises, seek an atmosphere of faith, be faithful in testimony, and you will not only be healed, but you will stay healed by the power of God. God has promised this, and God cannot lie.

CHAPTER 13
THE PRICE OF GOD'S MIRACLE WORKING POWER

My Personal Testimony

This chapter is a brief condensation of my book, The Price of God's Miracle Working Power. It includes my personal testimony of how God met with me while I was alone in a closet, fasting and praying. At that time, God told me personally of thirteen things in my life that stood between me and having His miracle-working power in my ministry. He also revealed to me that those very same things were also keeping multitudes of others from knowing His mighty power. The book is a mighty revelation from heaven and is thoroughly scriptural and doctrinally sound.

Immediately after my conversion at the age of twenty-three, God gave me a definite call to the ministry. That call was so definite that I never doubted the reality of it.

Being a Methodist, I knew nothing about the baptism of the Holy Ghost. In fact, before I was converted, I knew nothing about any part of the Bible. I couldn't even quote John 3:16 or name the Four Gospels. However, immediately after my conversion, my heart was hungry to know all that I could know of my Lord, and I began to search the Scriptures. I asked God to lead me to the scriptures that would bring me the greatest benefit. He began to reveal the truths of the baptism of the Holy Ghost, the signs following, the gifts of the Spirit, and the supernatural things of God.

It was not long until God led me into a Pentecostal church where I began to see, in a small measure, the blessings of God and a few of the manifestations of the Spirit. It was in these meetings that I became convinced of my need for the baptism of the Holy Spirit. I began to pray and seek God for that experience.

Thirty days after my conversion, in an Assembly of God camp meeting in Miami, Oklahoma, I was gloriously filled with the Holy Ghost and spoke in other tongues as the Spirit gave utterance.

I had read, Ye shall receive power, after that the Holy Ghost is come upon you (Acts 1:8), so I fully expected that, with the infilling of the Holy Ghost, I would immediately have power to heal the sick and perform miracles. But it did not take me long to realize that more was required than the baptism of the Holy Ghost, in order to consistently see these results. The baptism of the Spirit provides access to this power, but the gifts of the Spirit provide the channels for its operation. I immediately began to pray and seek the gifts of the Spirit. I felt that I must have power to heal the sick, for I knew that, according to the scriptures, God never called anyone to preach the gospel without also commissioning him to heal the sick.

Two years after my conversion, I married and began my ministry. In every revival meeting, I always scheduled at least two nights each week to preach divine healing and pray for the sick. During this time, we saw a large number of miraculous hearings as God honored the preaching of His Word. But I knew that God's plan included greater things for me, and I believed there would come a time when this plan would be a reality in my life.

The search for God's power

Many times, my wife and I searched the Scriptures together, becoming more convinced as we did so, that God's promises concerning the gifts of the Spirit, the signs following, healings, and miracles were meant for us today. It was clear that God had promised these things to us as His ministers. But it was also clear that we did not possess that power in the fullness that God had promised. We knew there must be a scriptural reason why we were lacking this power. Since God cannot lie, the fault had to be within us!

While pastoring my first church, I made up my mind that I must hear from heaven and know the reason why my ministry was not confirmed by signs and wonders. I felt sure that, if I fasted and prayed, God would reveal what stood between me His miracle-working power in my ministry. I was so hungry for the power of God in my life that I felt I could not stand in my pulpit and preach again until I had heard from God. I made up my mind that I would fast and pray until I got an answer, And, I told my wife of my plan.

It was then that I had the greatest battle of my life. Satan was determined that I should not fast and pray until God answered. Many times, he whipped me by tricking me out of my prayer closet. Satan knew that if I ever actually contacted God, it would hinder his evil cause. So he set out to do all in his power to keep me from making that contact.

Day after day, I went into the prayer closet, determined to stay until God spoke to me. Again and again, I came out without the answer. Again and again, my wife would say to me, "I thought you said this was the time you were going to stay until you got the answer." Then she would smile in her own sweet way, remembering that the spirit...is willing, but the flesh is weak (Matthew 26:41).

Again and again, I answered her, "Honey, I really meant to pray it through this time, but—!" It seemed there was always a reason why I couldn't stay in that closet until the answer came. I always justified myself by saying I would pray it through tomorrow. Things would be more favorable then.

The Lord encouraged my heart by calling to my attention how Daniel held on in fasting and prayer. He wrested the answer from the hands of Satan, although it took three weeks to do so (see Daniel 10:2,12).

The spiritual struggle

So the next day I was on my knees in the closet again. I had told my wife I would never come out until I heard from God, and I really thought I meant it. But a few hours later, when I began to smell the aroma of food being prepared, I was out of the closet and in the kitchen, inquiring, "What smells so delicious, Dear?"

At the table a few moments later, God spoke to my heart. I had only taken one bite of food, when I stopped. God had spoken to me. I knew in that moment that, until I wanted to hear from God more than anything else in the world—more than food and gratification of the flesh—I would never get my answer from God.

I quickly arose from the table and said to my wife, "Honey, I mean business with God this time! I'm going into the closet and I want you to lock me inside. I am going to stay there until I hear from God."

I had said this so many times before that she was beginning to wonder if I really could subdue the flesh long enough to defeat the devil. "Oh," she replied, "you'll be knocking for me to open the door in an hour or so." Nevertheless, I heard her lock the door from the outside, saying, "I'll let you out any time you knock."

I answered, "I'll not knock until I have the answer that I have wanted so long." At last, I had definitely made up my mind to stay there until I heard from God—no matter what the cost!

Hour after hour I battled the devil and the flesh in that closet! It seemed to me that days were slipping by and my progress was so slow. Many times I was tempted to give it all up and try to be satisfied without the answer - to just go on as I had been doing. But deep in my soul I knew I could never be satisfied doing that. I had tried it and found that it was not enough. So I kept on waiting.

A visitation from God

Then the glory of God began to fill the closet. As the interior of the closet began to grow light, I thought my wife had opened the door—but she had not. Jesus had opened the door of heaven and the closet was flooded with light, the light of the glory of God!

I do not know how long I was in the closet before this happened and it doesn't matter. I only know that I prayed until! The presence of God was so real and powerful that I felt I would die right there on my knees. It seemed that, if God came any closer, I could not stand it. Yet I wanted it and was determined to have it.

Was this my answer? Was God going to speak to me? Would He satisfy my longing heart at last, after these many years? I seemed to lose consciousness of everything except the mighty presence of God. I tried to see Him and then was afraid that I would, for suddenly I realized that should I see Him, I would die (see Exodus 33:20). Just His glorious presence was enough!

If only He would speak to me now! If He would just answer my question, "Lord, Why can't I heal the sick? Why can't I work miracles in Your name? Why do the signs not follow my ministry as they did that of Peter, John, and Paul?"

Then, like a whirlwind, I heard His voice! It was God! He was speaking to me! This was the glorious answer I had been waiting for since my conversion at the age of twenty-three!

In His presence, I felt like one of the small pebbles at the foot of the towering Rockies. I felt unworthy to even hear His voice. But He wasn't speaking to me because I was worthy, He was speaking because I was needy. Centuries ago, He had promised to supply that need, and this was the fulfillment of that promise.

It seemed that God was talking to me faster than any human could possibly speak - and faster than I could follow, mentally. My heart cried out, "Speak a little more slowly. I want to remember it all." Yet I knew I could never forget! God was giving me a list of the things, which stood between me and His power. After each new requirement was added to the list in my mind, there followed a brief explanation about the requirement and its importance.

If I had known there were so many things to remember, I would have brought a pencil and paper! I hadn't expected God to speak in such a definite way, giving me such a long list. I never dreamed I was falling so far short of the glory of God. I hadn't realized there were so many things in my life that generated doubt and hindered my faith.

As God continued to speak to me, I began to feel in my pockets for a pencil. At last I located one and began searching for a piece of paper. I couldn't find any. Suddenly I remembered the cardboard box filled with winter clothes that I was using for an altar. I would write on the box. Now I was ready!

The life-changing list

I asked the Lord to please start all over again and let me write the things down, one at a time. I asked Him to speak slowly so I could get it down on paper.

Once more, God started at the beginning and repeated the many things He had already revealed to me. As God spoke to me, I wrote down what He said.

When the last requirement was written on the list, God spoke once again. He said, "This is the answer. When you have placed on the altar of consecration and obedience the last thing on your list, ye shall not only heal the sick, but, in my name, shall ye cast out devils. Ye shall see mighty miracles as, in my name, ye preach the Word. For, behold, I give you power over all the power of the enemy."

God revealed to me the things that were hindrances to my ministry - the things that prevented Him from working with me, confirming the Word with signs following. They were the very same things, which were hindering thousands of others.

Now it began to grow darker in the closet. I felt His mighty power begin to lift. For a few more moments, His presence lingered...and then I was alone. Alone, yet not alone.

I trembled under the mighty lingering presence of God. In the darkness, I fumbled at the bottom of the cardboard box, tearing off the list I had written down. In my hand, I held the list. At last, here was the price I must pay in order to have the power of God in my life and ministry—the price tag for the miracle-working power of God!

Frantically I pounded on the locked door. Again and again I pounded. Finally I heard my wife coming. She opened the door and the moment she saw me, she knew I'd been with God. Her first words were, "You've got the answer!"

"Yes, honey. God has paid me a visit from heaven, and here is the answer."

In my hand was the old brown piece of card board with the answer that had cost so many hours of fasting and prayer, waiting, and yes, believing!

My wife and I sat down at the table with the list before us. As I told her the story and we went down the list together, we both wept. There were thirteen items on the list when I came out of the closet, but I erased the last two before showing the list to my wife. These were too personal for even her to know. She has never asked me about them because she realizes it must remain between me and God.

The other eleven requirements make up the contents of my book, The Price of God's Miracle Working Power. There is one entire chapter devoted to each of the eleven requirements. If you, too, long for the manifestation of the mighty power of God in your own life and ministry, be sure to read this book!

Since God spoke to me that day in the closet, many pages have been torn from the calendar. In fact, many calendars have been replaced by new ones. As time has passed, I have marked the requirements from my list, one by one. The list grew smaller and smaller as I shouted the victory over Satan and marked off one after another!

Finally, I was down to the last two requirements. Satan said to me, "You've marked off eleven, but here are two you'll never mark off! I've got you whipped."

But, by the grace of God, I told the devil he was a liar. If God said I could mark them all off, He would help me do it! But it was quite some time before I was able to mark off the last two.

I will never forget the day when I looked over my list and found that there was only one thing left! Praise God, if I could mark that one off, I could claim the promise God had made to me.

I had to claim that promise! Millions were sick and afflicted—beyond the help of medical science. Someone must bring deliverance to them. God had called me to take deliverance to the people and God has called every minister of the gospel to do the same! (See Ezekiel 34:1–4).

Many times as I traveled across the states, God had poured out His Spirit on my meetings. However, I knew that when I marked that last item from my list, I would see miracles such as I had never seen before. In the meantime, I would patiently strive toward victory, trusting God to help me until the victory came. I knew that, when victory was mine, God would be glorified and others, too, would be encouraged to seek for His power.

A great moving of God's power

As I wrote this book, I was conducting a "Back to God Healing Revival" in Oakland, California. Many said it was the greatest revival in the history of Oakland. Hundreds said they had never witnessed such a dynamic moving of the power of God. Night after night, the waves of divine glory swept over the congregation. Many testified of being healed while sitting in their seats. Again and again, we felt the mighty power of God settling over the meeting. People rose to their feet to testify of instant healings - some of which were visibly miraculous, such as outward tumors disappearing and cripples being made whole.

I felt goiters disappear at the touch of my hand, in Jesus' name!

There were many shouts of victory as the blind received their sight. One woman testified, "It was like coming out of the dark into the sunlight."

We prayed for a woman with throat trouble. After a few moments, she hurried to the ladies rest room. After returning to the auditorium, she testified that, after prayer, something came loose in her throat and came up into her mouth. She had hurried to the rest room to dispose of it. It was some kind of foreign growth (probably cancer), whitish-orange in color.

Ruptures as large as a person's fist disappeared overnight. Cancer, deafness, tumor, goiter, sugar diabetes—

every known disease and many unknown—disappeared as, in the name of Jesus, we laid hands on the sick. In many cases, healings were verified by doctors' reports and x-rays.

We stand in holy awe and marvel at the miracle-working power of God. It moved, night after night, from the beginning of the meeting. Hundreds were delivered from the power of the enemy—saved, healed, or filled with the Spirit.

In this meeting, it was impossible to have what is generally termed as a "healing line." At least ninety percent of those we laid hands on were immediately prostrated under the mighty power of God. Some danced a few steps or moved drunkenly under the power of the Spirit before falling (see Jeremiah 23:9). Under those circumstances, it was impossible to have people march on after prayer.

Many would brand this as fanaticism, but it is not! It is the mighty power of God moving upon the people. It is the same miraculous power that caused John to fall at his feet as dead (Revelation 1:17).

Many say that the most outstanding thing about this meeting was that such a large percentage of the sick received miraculous deliverances. It would be a conservative estimate to say that at least ninety percent—or even more—of those prayed for were marvelously healed.

One night's service was designated "Holy Ghost Night." The auditorium was packed to the doors, with people sitting on the altar benches. Eternity alone will reveal the number of people who were filled, or refilled, with the Spirit. We announced that, in this service, hands would be laid upon seekers for the infilling of the Spirit, according to Acts 8:17. After the sermon, all who had not already been filled during the service came forward for prayer. With only a few exceptions, everyone we touched in the name of Jesus, fell prostate. What an unusual sight - to stand on the platform afterwards, and look upon the many "slain of the Lord." They were in every available altar space and even down the aisles! Sweeter yet was the sound of the heavenly music as voices joined in united praise to God. The Holy Spirit filled obedient believers and they began to speak in new tongues and magnify God (see Mark 16:17; Acts 10:46).

Although I do not claim to possess the gift of healing, hundreds were miraculously healed in this meeting, as well as in following campaigns. I do not claim to possess a single gift of the Spirit, or to have power to impart any gift to others, yet all the gifts of the Spirit were in operation, night after night. God confirmed His Word with signs following!

Victory, at last!

Why did I see such a change in the results of my ministry? You ask WHY? Have you not guessed?

At last, the final item was marked off the list! Hallelujah! Many times, I almost gave up hope of ever being able to mark that last one off. But, at last, it is gone! By God's grace, gone forever!

With the marking off of the last requirement on my list came the fulfillment of God's promise. The sick were healed, devils were cast out, and mighty miracles were seen, in the name of Jesus, as His Word was preached!

Are you hungry for the power of God in your own life? Then get alone with God. Seek Him with an open heart and ask Him to show you the things that stand between you and Him (read Isaiah 59:1–2). Do not stop until you are victorious over everything that generates doubt and unbelief!

This is not a "magic formula"—it is not an easy way, but it is one that works. It may often seem to be a hard and lonely road, but God has promised in His Word that, if it is followed, miracle-working power will be ours!

If you are truly hungry for more of the power of God in your life, get a copy of my book, "The Price of God's Miracle-Working Power."

Thus concludes your book, which is one from our pocket book collection. These are intentionally printed in a smaller size for you to carry, read anywhere, and share!

Be sure to visit us online for more of the best Christian books ever written, including a wide variety of eBooks and full-sized reads.

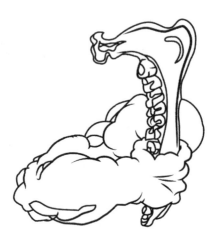

http://JawboneDigital.com/pocket

Made in the USA
Columbia, SC
16 September 2021

45574940R00065